134

THIS IS a pioneering work that provides a complete presentation of the application of computer technology to data processing of state and local governments.

After a comprehensive analysis of the data used by state and local governments, this book develops a long-range system for using automatic equipment to handle these data—the *Unified Information System*.

Designed to reduce duplication in the collection, storage, and processing of data, and to increase the accessibility and usefulness of data, the system presented in this book illustrates how the application of computer techniques can improve local and state governmental operations.

Beginning with a description of the equipment used for computer processing, this book traces the functions and organizational structures of state and local governments, and the data used in their operations.

It then introduces the organization of the *Unified Information System*, detailing every aspect of an Information Center, its organization and services.

The activities of the *System* are developed to include the phases of data input—collection methods, criteria and media, as well as operations—and output, communications, storage, and processing.

The costs and benefits of the *Unified Information System* are developed, and methods of im-

A Data Processing System
for State and Local Governments

PRENTICE-HALL INTERNATIONAL, INC., *London*
PRENTICE-HALL OF AUSTRALIA, PTY., LTD., *Sydney*
PRENTICE-HALL OF CANADA, LTD., *Toronto*
PRENTICE-HALL FRANCE, S.A.R.L., *Paris*
PRENTICE-HALL OF INDIA PRIVATE LIMITED, *New Delhi*
PRENTICE-HALL OF JAPAN, INC., *Tokyo*
PRENTICE-HALL DE MEXICO, S.A., *Mexico City*

A Data Processing System
for State and Local Governments

Edward F. R. Hearle

Raymond J. Mason

The RAND Corporation

Prentice-Hall, Inc.   *Englewood Cliffs, New Jersey*

PRENTICE-HALL, INC.
ENGLEWOOD CLIFFS, N.J.

LIBRARY OF CONGRESS
CATALOG CARD NO.: 63-21039

PRINTED IN THE
UNITED STATES OF AMERICA

C

PREFACE

This book is the result of two years of research conducted by the authors on data processing for state and local governments. The objective of this research was to provide government officials and other interested persons with an analysis of long-range possibilities and preferred approaches to utilizing advanced data processing equipment to support the functions of state and local agencies.

Because of limited resources, state and local governments themselves are in a difficult position to undertake such research, and it was felt that an independent study would be useful, particularly in taking intergovernmental considerations into account.

The authors wish to acknowledge the generous assistance of the many state and local government officials who provided us with both information and insights. We further wish to acknowledge the help of John A. Postley, who was active in the initial stages of the study while at The RAND Corporation. Several of our RAND colleagues also made helpful comments during the research, especially Anthony J. Dowkont on communications and Solomon L. Pollack on input. Valuable comments and suggestions on the manuscript were made by Donald Axelrod of the New York State Government and Robert H. Gregory, Will Harriss, Stephen A. Marglin, Fred T. Moore, and Richard L. Van Horn, all of The RAND Corporation.

The study has been supported by The RAND Corporation as part of its program of RAND-sponsored research. In addition to its work for the United States Air Force and other government agencies, RAND frequently sponsors, with its own funds, other research projects important to the national security and public welfare. The results are published in the hope that they contribute to wider understanding of important public problems.

Edward F. R. Hearle

Raymond J. Mason

Santa Monica, California

CONTENTS

CHAPTER ONE

INTRODUCTION

During the past few years, two developments have caused state and local governments, like businesses, to become increasingly interested in improving their data processing operations: first, rapid growth in the activities of these governmental units requires the handling of expanding volumes of data; and second, major technological advances have been made in data processing equipment.

State and local governments have responded to these developments mainly by mechanizing well-understood clerical procedures, such as payroll preparation, tax and appropriation accounting, and utility billing, or by substituting electronic systems for existing punch card procedures in such functions as licensing drivers and keeping unemployment insurance records. Little basic research has been done on the nature of the data used by state and local governments or on the design of comprehensive systems to serve their long-range needs. It is to these problems that this study is addressed.

Several ground rules have guided our research. First, the study focuses on the *total complex of functions* performed by state and local governments rather than on the operations of any specific agency. Our analysis, therefore, is unconstrained by the organizational problems that frequently dominate the design of systems for a particular city, state, or county. We have searched for common characteristics and principles relevant to many state and local government organizations.

Second, the study is *conceptual* rather than procedural. Its aim is not to serve as a handbook or check list for answering such questions as, "How may a computer be justified in a state highway department?" or, "How can a police department use electronic data processing (EDP) equipment?" We are not primarily concerned with questions of equipment selection or with describing current applications as they are traditionally defined. Rather, we believe the answers to such questions will emerge from our broader analysis of the information used to perform the entire range of state and local government functions. Therefore, our focus is on the design of an improved system that state and local governments could use in handling information.

Third, the study is *futuristic*. It is heavily oriented toward the design of systems that will accommodate both the new technologies of data processing and the rapidly expanding functions of state and local governments. Thus, although it suggests specific actions for today, the bulk of the analysis is directed toward formulating a long-range system suitable for implementation in the 1970-75 period.

Fourth, the study is concerned primarily with *data* processing, not document or record handling; nor does it emphasize scientific or engineering computing, although the system described in Chapters 5, 6, and 7 provides capability for such applications.

Chapter 2 describes the characteristics and capabilities of data processing equipment. Since we believe advances in data processing technology will enable state and local governments to take a fresh and fundamentally different approach to data systems, we have delineated foreseeable equipment capability. Because data systems serve organizations, Chapter 3 discusses state and local governments: their functions, structures, relationships, and prospects. Chapter 4 takes up the data that these governments handle in performing their functions, and the analysis of these data leads us, in Chapters 5, 6, and 7, to propose the Unified Information System as a long-range goal for state and local governments. Finally, we discuss steps that agencies can take today, both to improve present data systems and to provide logical transition to the Unified Information System envisioned for the 1970's. The appendixes provide further detail about state and local government data, present several major principles of data system design to guide agencies today, comment on equipment evaluation and selection, and furnish references for additional guidance.

Before turning to a description of data processing equipment, we should like to emphasize that we recognize data processing considerations are not the dominant concern in many government functions. We are addressing ourselves to what is primarily a procedural question within government agencies; however, we believe that improved systems for handling data can significantly improve the execution of the policies which the data systems should be designed to serve. Thus, although data processing is not in itself a matter of major concern in the formulation of public policy, it should rate high on the scale of administrative concern within the management priorities of state and local government officials.

CHAPTER TWO

DATA PROCESSING EQUIPMENT

Equipment for handling information, including such prosaic devices as the pen, the typewriter, and the bookkeeping machine, has existed for many years.[1] The special term "data processing equipment" applies primarily to punch card machines and to electronic computers and the devices associated with them. Electronic data processing equipment is important to state and local governments because it enables them to handle increasingly greater amounts of information in far more ways than is possible with any prior equipment.

Before discussing the information-handling equipment that constitutes an electronic computer system, let us examine the five major phases of any information system, whether manual or automatic. These five phases are *input*, to acquire data and enter them into the system; *storage*, to file data either temporarily or permanently; *processing*, to manipulate data according to specified rules; *output*, to present the results of the processing or the status of any data stored in the system; and *communications*, to move the data from one point in the system to another. In the following discussion, the term "data processing" is often used to cover all five of these phases. We use the terms "data processing," "data handling," "information processing," and "information handling" interchangeably. A data processing system is a comprehensive and interrelated grouping of procedures and equipment designed to handle data in order to achieve a specific goal.

The main hardware elements of a data processing system, depicted in Fig. 1, can be discussed according to the five major phases defined above. A subphase, *inquiry*, is presented separately because it involves a combination of both input and output at a single location. In this discussion, we shall outline the current devices used for each of these phases and suggest

---

[1] This chapter discusses the general capability of data processing equipment. References to descriptions of specific equipment are contained in Appendix D.

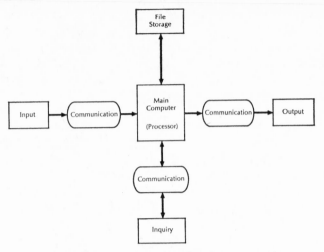

Fig. 1. Main hardware elements of a data processing system

the technological capability we believe will be available during the 1970-75 period.

INPUT DEVICES

Input devices collect data and enter them into the system. To process data, the equipment must receive them in an understandable form. People need only about 50 or 60 different symbols (numbers, letters, and special characters) to convey all the information they use; the symbols are combined into words, sentences, and other complete expressions of thought. Punch card systems represent these symbols by holes punched in cards. The presence or absence of a hole in a specific place is interpreted by the equipment to represent a specific character. Electronic devices receive information in the form of electrical impulses or from holes punched in paper or cards. The presence or absence of a specific impulse or hole in a specific place is interpreted by the machine to represent a particular particle of information.

At present the punch card is the commonest method of input to mechanized information-handling systems. Usually the card is keypunched from an original source-document, such as a payroll time sheet, building permit, or crime report. The key punch machine has keys like those on a typewriter. When struck, they activate punches which make holes in cards. Other equipment in the system later "reads" these holes and thus receives information. The main drawbacks of key punch input are that it is slow and costly and subject to transcription error because a person must first interpret source documents and then keypunch his interpretation. The card he produces, however, is an excellent unit record within the capacity it has for carrying information. Since most punch cards can carry only 80 or 90 characters of information, it often takes several cards to make a complete record.

Devices for reducing manual effort in data input have developed rapidly in the last several years. For example, credit-card templates with raised letters now enable the automatic scanning of characters printed from the impression of the raised letters. Magnetic ink has been used for special characters printed on bank checks. Devices "read" these magnetically sensitized characters and thus reduce manual transcription effort. The use of paper tape punched with holes as a byproduct of accounting machine and typewriter operations is also increasing. This tape is often produced automatically as a direct byproduct of the normal key stroke or machine operation involved in another process, such as ledger entry or adding machine totaling.

When the punch card itself can serve as the original source-document, "mark-sensing," or the use of an electrographic pencil to place marks in specified positions on the punch card, is widely used today in utility meter field records, civil service examination answer sheets, and police field incident reports. Machines can automatically translate these marks into punched holes. A variation of the mark-sense card is a hand-portable punch with which a person can punch holes in the card manually. The data represented by these marks or holes are then read automatically.

The 1960 Federal Census used a specialized input technique called "FOSDIC" (Film Optical Sensing Device for Input to Computer) which enabled the field enumerator to mark answers to questions in ordinary pencil lead in prespecified places on large forms. The forms were then microphotographed; by passing an electronic beam through the photographic image, information was read by the positions of the marked spots. This device brought about major reductions in the clerical conversion of data from source documents to electronic storage files.

With other devices, data can be collected at remote input points and transmitted automatically to a central point. Using this method, certain fixed data, such as date, time, and place, can be automatically recorded by these devices, and employees can manually enter such variable data as hours spent on a particular project or type of license requested. Both fixed and variable data are automatically transmitted to the central location for storage, processing, or both. Thus, all these devices are designed to reduce manual effort in data input.

Other input devices currently under development and in the basic research stage are also designed for this purpose. Major advances in electronic devices that automatically read printed matter are certain to be made during the next decade. For example, optical reading of typewritten characters is already available, and automatic reading of variable type fonts is forthcoming. Although it is unlikely that hand*writing* will be reliably read electronically in the 1970-75 period, it is likely that the hand*printing* of millions of people will be reliably read by automatic devices. In summary, there will be great variety and flexibility in the input devices and methods available in the 1970-75 period.

This promise is significant for many state and local governments, since one of their main data processing problems is the efficient collection of large amounts of data. As governments expand their data collection programs, improved input devices will relieve a problem that would be almost insurmountable under manual systems. Small as well as large agencies will benefit from these improved input devices because they will be available in a wide range of costs and capabilities.

Output Devices

Output devices present data either in the form in which they are stored in the system or in a form resulting from a particular type of processing. Printed output is the most familiar and typically takes the form of such documents as checks, licenses, tax bills, precinct lists, and various aggregations of data into reports for management review. Devices for data output in printed form have existed for many years, and are increasing in both speed and flexibility. Today, mechanical printers operate at a wide range of speeds up to 1200 lines per minute, and the trend is toward even faster and cheaper printing through such techniques as photochemical processes, which now operate at rates up to 6000 lines per minute. Faster printed output will have a major impact on several government functions, particularly those concerned with distributing, in a short period of time, such documents as tax bills or motor vehicle registration certificates.

In addition to printed output, equipment is coming onto the market for displaying digital data on screens for one-time review. Besides conventional narrative, numerical data can be shown graphically and photographed for a permanent record. For example, a screen can display a map image of a city on which the locations of events such as fires, building regulation infractions, or traffic accidents are shown from data stored in the system. Even engineering data, such as locations of subsurface utility conduits in a street, can be graphically displayed as an image composed of a multitude of plotted dots.

In addition to devices for input and output of digital data, equipment is becoming available for scanning documents, transmitting the facsimile image, and reproducing it at another location. For example, one device now permits 600 page-size documents to be scanned, transmitted, and printed in an hour. It is even possible to receive vocal output through the use of prerecorded messages which are selected by a computer. Devices for supplying output data in many formats will increase in speed and flexibility during the next decade and will be able to accommodate any of the requirements of state and local governments by 1970-75.

INQUIRY DEVICES

Inquiry devices provide a combination of input and output. They are the means of requesting and receiving desired information from a central processing or storage location. Inquiries can be made by any of the methods available for input, and the answer can be supplied by any of the output devices. The most common inquiry devices provide for keyboard input and printed output.

Several extensive inquiry systems are currently under development for airlines. The need for many remote inquiry locations to communicate with a central storage record concerning flights and seat availability is great in the airline industry because the cost of not selling an available seat is relatively high. Systems under development will permit inquiries from over 1000 reservation agents all over the country to be transferred to a single computer center which will maintain flight and seat reservation information. One system to be installed in 1963 is designed to accommodate 85,000 daily telephone calls, 30,000 daily requests for fare quotations, 40,000 daily passenger reservations, 30,000 daily queries to and from other airlines, and 20,000 daily ticket sales.[2] It generally takes less than three seconds between inquiry by an agent at any location in the country and his receipt of an answer. Inquiry devices will develop increased speed, sophistication, and ability to handle multiple inquiries simultaneously during the next decade. These devices will simplify the communication of data between multiple remote locations and a central location.

COMMUNICATIONS

Communication devices, media, and techniques permit data to be moved from one point in the system to another. Advances in communications capability over the next decade will be spectacular. Data can be transmitted over either land lines or microwave facilities. Both common-carrier communication networks and privately owned or leased facilities

---

[2] The American Airlines' SABRE System, described by W. R. Plugge and M. N. Perry in *Proceedings of the Western Joint Computer Conference,* Vol. 19, 1961, p. 593.

will be available. Today the common-carrier commercial network can transmit digital data over conventional telephone circuits at rates of nearly 300 characters per second. Already, special leased facilities can transmit over 65,000 characters of digital data per second. Terminal devices connected to both ends of the communications circuit convert the signals into a form acceptable to the data handling equipment at either end. This conversion process is entirely automatic and highly reliable. Various automatic self-checking routines can be included to minimize error. Both speed and reliability of transmission will improve, although present transmission capability exceeds any foreseeable requirements of state and local governments.

STORAGE DEVICES

In manual systems, data are stored by writing letters, numbers, and symbols on pieces of paper and then filing them. In punch card systems, information is stored in the form of holes punched into cards. Electronic devices store large volumes of data on magnetic tapes, discs, or cards in the form of magnetized impulses on the surface of the storage medium. Present devices have storage capacities exceeding 700 million characters of information, with access to any set of characters in less than one second. The trend in large-volume electronic storage media is toward greater capacity and lower access time to the stored information. There are promising technological developments in magnetic media with greater density for "packing" the bits of information; other techniques using thin film, thermoplastic, photochemical, and cryogenic devices may provide even further storage and access capabilities.

By 1970 there will be a technological capability to store billions of characters of data with access time measured in seconds. This capability is directly relevant to many state and local government functions that are concerned with the storage of large volumes of data. Timely access to these data is often as important as their efficient storage. Law enforcement agencies, for example, frequently need rapid access to data on persons. Another example is the duplicate records that are often maintained in branch offices of large departments because there is no efficient way to gain access to a central file.[3] This duplication is costly because several files must continually be updated. By 1970, technological advances will have greatly reduced such problems, and present concern about random versus serial storage of information will become less significant as access

---

[3] By "file" we mean an ordered grouping of records containing data, not the physical storage device in which papers are kept.

time diminishes. In fact, all required data can be made available virtually as fast as they are needed.

In some state and local government functions, documents, as distinct from data, are of major importance for both legal and administrative reasons. Although the data from the documents are used in performing most functions, document images themselves must occasionally be made available. This is true of legal documents filed in court cases, and of permits and applications involved in numerous administrative actions. In addition to devices for storing digital data, rapid advances in techniques for storing documents and document images are inevitable. The size of the document image will be radically reduced so that increasingly more images can be stored in a given space.

Systems for retrieving documents and/or their images are also becoming more advanced and sophisticated, so that long narrative records, maps, or pictures can be delivered automatically from storage in a few seconds.

Processing

In an electronic system, data are processed by computers that manipulate them according to specified rules. Such manipulations involve comparisons, aggregations, calculations, and other decision rules, all of which are executed logically and rapidly. Present computers carry out arithmetical and logical operations in millionths of a second; before 1970, however, speeds will increase to billionths of a second. Such technological advances will facilitate what is often called "on line" or "real time" data processing, which is the processing of data by automatic devices so that the output of information is provided without significant delay.

Computers are also being given greater capability for performing several unrelated processing operations at essentially the same time. For example, it will be possible for automatic equipment to compute tax bills for a county assessor and at the same time record encumbrances in a municipal public works appropriation record and make elaborate engineering calculations to determine the size, location, and design of a contemplated storm drain for a state engineering agency. Because most state and local government functions require relatively simple processing—as contrasted to extensive calculations for solving many scientific problems—the prospective capability of computer processing exceeds any foreseeable state and local government requirements.

All components of data processing system equipment will have increasingly greater versatility. The building-block principle of equipment design promises to continue, thus enabling modules of equipment to be "plugged in" to each other for purposes of expanding a system capability. Modular equipment tends to lessen equipment obsolescence because additional, rather than replacement, devices can be employed. Original equipment procurement can also be limited to the requireents of the initial system. In summary, data processing equipment during the next decade will develop greater speed, versatility, and modular capabilities for expansion.

PROGRAMMING

The computer must be given detailed instructions on how to process data. Translating decision rules and processing instructions from ordinary English to language that the electronic equipment can "understand" is called programming. In the early days of computers, programming was complex and costly. In fact, programming has often cost more than the equipment itself. However, in the next decade, these costs will decrease significantly. Already, "business-oriented languages" which are becoming available enable the equipment user to specify in simple, standardized language the operations he wants the computer system to perform. The translation of these instructions into programs and codes for computer execution is almost automatic. These *user*-oriented, as distinct from *machine*-oriented, languages will increase in simplicity and usefulness over the next few years. In fact, by 1970, the user can expect to specify, in carefully written ordinary English and conventional flow charts or tabular logic, the decision rules and processing instructions he wishes the computer system to execute. This does not mean that government agencies should forget about training personnel to use computer systems; proper understanding of the capabilities and limitations of computer systems is necessary for their effective use. Such training should, however, focus more on the design of data systems which utilize automatic equipment rather than on the writing of detailed machine instructions. If a data system is properly designed, the computer programming will be relatively straight-forward, and many of its processes will be performed automatically by 1970.

CONCLUSION

By 1970 to 1975, the technological capabilities of information-handling equipment will be sufficient to handle any foreseeable data processing task required by state and local governments. Of course, using this equipment effectively will not be a simple or trivial task; a major effort will be required to design data systems that can fully exploit the equipment. As computers acquire greater capability to handle information, managers must seek to understand and to specify in more explicit terms the role of information in various state and local government functions. This under-standing and specification must extend beyond solely clerical procedures to the more complex use of information in management planning and control decisions. In the chapters that follow, we describe the organizations such data systems serve, identify the information they use, and suggest how a significantly improved system could be designed to handle this in-formation in the 1970-75 period.

CHAPTER THREE

STATE AND LOCAL GOVERNMENTS

Data systems must be designed to fit the characteristics and require-ments of the organizations they serve. This chapter discusses the current and prospective characteristics of state and local governments and the relevance of these traits to data system design.

State and local governments in the United States are among the major enterprises of the nation. In 1960, one in every nine employed persons worked for a unit of state or local government: state, county, township, city, or district. Collectively, these units employ nearly three times as many persons as does the Federal government and currently spend over $60 billion annually, thus exceeding our national security expenditures by several billion dollars. The personnel and expenditure growth of state and local governments versus the Federal government is compared in Table 1. From 1950 to 1960, state and local government expenditures increased from 9.8 to 12.1 per cent of the gross national product. Thus, the magnitude of state and local government operations is both large and expanding.

TABLE 1

COMPARISON OF FEDERAL VERSUS STATE AND LOCAL EMPLOYEES AND EXPENDITURES

Year	State and Local Governments		Federal Government	
	Employees	Expenditures	Employees [a]	Expenditures
1950	4,285,000	$27,905,000,000	2,117,000	$39,544,000,000
1960	6,387,000	60,999,000,000	2,421,000	76,539,000,000
Increase	49%	119%	14%	94%

[a] Excludes armed forces personnel.

Source: U. S. Department of Commerce, Bureau of the Census, *Statistical Abstract of the United States, 1962*, Washington, D.C., 1962.

These operations involve large volumes of data, and even larger volumes are inevitable with the increase of population and government services. Designing systems to handle these data requires a knowledge both of the purposes for which the data are used and of the organizations that use them. In government these purposes are customarily called functions.

FUNCTIONS

Functions are simply the responsibilities that society has assigned to state and local government agencies. Table 2 is a comprehensive grouping of these functions.

TABLE 2

STATE AND LOCAL GOVERNMENT FUNCTIONS

Correction-Probation
  Correctional institutions
  Parole
  Probation

Culture-Recreation
  Libraries
  Museums, art galleries, arboreta
  Parks and beaches
  Recreation

Education

Natural Resources
  Agriculture
  Fish and game
  Forests
  Gas and oil
  Mines
  Soil
  Water

Protection to Persons and Property
  Animal regulation
  Civil defense
  Emergency hospital
  Fire
  National Guard
  Police

  Structural regulation
  Urban renewal

Public Health
  Environmental sanitation
  Laboratories
  Mental health
  Preventive services
  Vital records

Public Welfare and Security
  Categorical aid
  Compensation insurance
  Employment services
  General relief
  Indigent medical care
  Institution regulation
  Youth services

Public Works
  Assessments
  Contract administration
  Engineering, construction, maintenance
  Map records and technical data
  Standards and testing
  Traffic engineering

Regulation and Licensing
  Agriculture
  Air pollution
  Alcoholic beverages
  Charity solicitation
  Corporations
  Industrial relations
  Insurance companies
  Motor vehicles
  Private investment
  Professions and vocations
  Public utilities
  Tobacco sales
  Vehicle operators
  Weights and measures

Sanitation
  Lot and weed cleaning
  Refuse collection and disposal

General Government
  Administrative management
  Coroner—Public administrator
  Elections administration
  Financial administration
  Judicial services
  Legal services
  Legislative services
  Planning
  Property management
  Recorder
  Revenue collection
  Zoning

Proprietary
  Airports
  Bus—streetcar
  Electricity distribution
  Gas distribution
  Harbors
  Water distribution

This table lists only the major functions and primary subfunctions. Each subfunction can be divided into activities and these, in turn, divided into subactivities, down to six or seven levels of detail.

The first relevant trait of these functions is their dependence on data. Several—notably those involving licensing, registration, taxing, and legal recordkeeping—are dominated by data processing considerations. Much of the data processing in state and local government involves large volumes of transactions, each relatively simple but together comprising a formidable data processing task, especially for larger agencies.

The second salient feature of these functions is their diversity, which has led to the organization of functions into departments and to data systems built around department functions. In most state and local governments, one normally finds separate department systems for welfare data, police data, health data, and agricultural data. Data systems encompassing an entire governmental unit such as a state or a city are unusual except for some jurisdiction-wide accounting systems.

ORGANIZATIONAL STRUCTURES

The organizational characteristics of governmental units are as important to data system design as are their functions. Table 3 identifies the six major types of state and local governmental units and shows the number

TABLE 3

NUMBER OF STATE AND LOCAL GOVERNMENTAL UNITS

Type of Unit	Number of Units			
	1962	1957	1952	1942
States	50	48	48	48
Counties	3,043	3,047	3,049	3,050
Cities	17,997	17,183	16,778	16,220
Townships and towns	17,144	17,198	17,202	18,919
School districts	34,678	50,446	56,346	108,579
Special districts	18,323	14,405	12,319	8,299
Total	91,235	102,327	105,742	155,115

Source: U. S. Department of Commerce, Bureau of the Census, *Governments in the United States,* Washington, D.C., 1957, and "Governmental Units in 1962," *1962 Census of Governments.*

of units within each type. The number of state and local governments decreased by 41 per cent in the 20 years covered in Table 3, largely through the consolidation of school districts. Special districts, on the other hand, substantially increased. There is no reason to believe that these numerical trends will change. In the following discussion of state and local government organizations, it should also be remembered that there are structural differences in various parts of the country. Our purpose is to point up major characteristics of these governments that have a significant effect on data systems.

States

In the American system, the state is historically the prime unit of government. Although its role has declined in relation to the Federal government, it dominates within the framework of state and local government. To a large extent, local units are able to do only what the state government authorizes them to do.

State governments are divided into the familiar three branches: executive, legislative, and judicial. The executive branch, where most data processing activities take place, is headed by a governor and groups of administrative departments. (See Fig. 2, a simplified organization chart of a representative state government.) Typically, state governments have departments, boards, commissions, and agencies with various degrees of independence from the direct control of the governor. Several important state officers besides the governor are usually elected directly by the people and, therefore, are not subject to administrative control by the chief

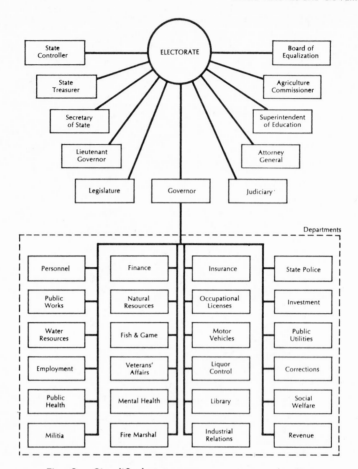

Fig. 2.   Simplified state government organization

executive. These officers include the attorney general, superintendent of public instruction, members of boards of equalization, and agricultural commissioners. Other departments whose directors are appointed by the governor often have a board or commission which has administrative authority over them.

The presence of such elected officials and semiautonomous boards and commissions severely restricts the governor's ability to control and integrate functions of state government and makes it more difficult to achieve state-wide objectives on a comprehensive basis. This characteristic, like that of functional diversity, reinforces the traditional departmental independence of state data systems.

Counties

Historically, counties have served as administrative subdivisions of the state to facilitate local performance of state functions. Especially in rural regions, counties have become the most familiar level of government to the average citizen and have undertaken functions relating to his everyday life, such as health, welfare, agriculture, land ownership records, vital statistics, road maintenance, and the local court system.

Counties are circumscribed in their functions and operations by state laws which often specify detailed office procedures as well as organization and policy. The sizes of counties vary markedly, and there are major differences between rural and urban counties; these two facts significantly affect the way they operate and lead to differences in data systems accordingly.

In recent years counties have increasingly assumed additional functions under county, as contrasted to state, control. These functions are usually initiated by the local citizenry and, although often requiring permissive state legislation, they frequently involve less state supervision than do the more traditional state functions that have been decentralized to counties for several decades.

Counties are generally governed by an elected legislative body but seldom have central executives; typically the people directly elect a host of administrative officials as well. Such officers often include an assessor, auditor, clerk, coroner, constable, district attorney, justice of the peace, public administrator, public defender, recorder, sheriff, superintendent of schools, tax collector, license collector, and treasurer. (See Fig. 3.)

Towns and Townships

Towns developed in New England in the early colonial days and were organized primarily for the protection of the settlers. They continue today, largely in New England, as a highly democratic unit of local government, performing many of the typical functions of cities. Township government is organized along the lines of the New England towns and functions in primarily rural areas as a subdivision of the county.

As improved communications and transportation have enabled people to deal directly with the county seat for county services, rural townships have declined. However, several urban townships still flourish, often as electoral units to provide representation on the governing body of the county in which the township is located. In some areas urban townships continue to provide roads and have almost all the same powers granted to municipal corporations. In some urban fringe areas, townships remain

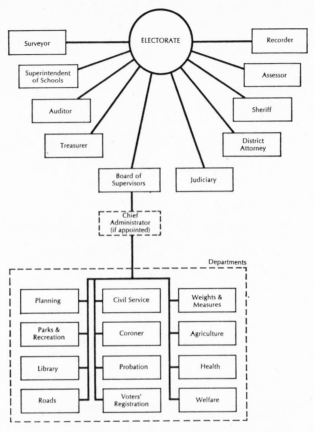

Fig. 3. Simplified county government organization

an important source of government services outside the boundaries of the city. Thus, for purposes of data system design, towns can be considered similar to cities, and townships similar to counties.

Cities

Cities are perhaps the most familiar form of local government and have, in many respects, the greatest autonomy. Some operate under charters from their state legislatures granting them special independence. Others operate under general state law which applies uniformly to all cities in a "general law" class. In organization, cities are often categorized by the nature of their executive branches: "strong mayor" or "weak mayor" or "council-manager" are typical terms used to describe the administrative organization of municipalities. Cities universally also have a legislative body and often, though not always, are responsible for the judiciary within the municipal boundaries. A representative organization of a small city is shown in Fig. 4.

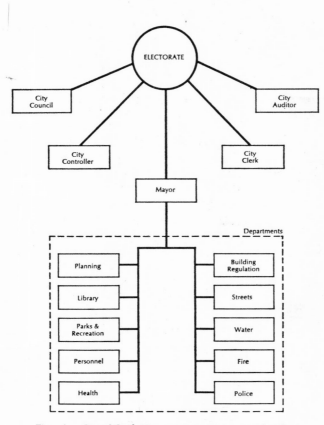

Fig. 4. Simplified city government organization

Cities perform an array of functions less diverse than those performed by counties, and generally have a more integrated administrative structure than do counties or states. The number of elected officials, besides the legislative body, is generally smaller in cities, and power is often more centralized in the executive and the legislative bodies. Accordingly, data systems tend to be more integrated across departments than in states or counties, although the amount of integration is still insignificant.

Districts

The most numerous governmental unit is the district. The school districts are decidedly the largest in number and expenditures. As Table 3 indicates, however, the number of school districts is declining rapidly because of consolidation of smaller districts into unified and union school districts.

Other districts are generally designated "special districts." In 1957, the functions performed by special districts were, in order of greatest frequency, fire protection, soil conservation, drainage, cemetery, housing, urban water supply, and highways.

Special districts have a substantial degree of independence from other units of state and local government and often have their own sources of revenue. Most of them perform a single function. Many special districts have been created to perform functions which cities and counties have been legally, politically, or financially unable to undertake. Such special districts are generally managed by an elected board of directors, which is composed of the same persons who are responsible for the city or county government or of persons directly elected by the citizens or constituent governmental units within the district boundaries. Their executive officer is usually appointed and has general management authority. Although school districts have decreased in number, the special district form of local government has experienced continuing growth, and probably will continue to expand as a major means of providing local government service. Because of their single-function characteristic, districts have generally developed more cohesive data systems than are typical in states, counties, and cities.

INTERGOVERNMENTAL RELATIONS

Although these separate units of government are independent organizations, their interrelationships are often as important as their unilateral activities. All units of local government are to some extent political subdivisions of the state and are largely subject to state laws prescribing their organization and operations.

Relationships between the state government and local units of government develop in several ways. The least formal is an informational relationship, generally involving periodic reports on financial transactions and other activities by local units to the state. State agencies, in turn, furnish information and advice to local units and render technical aid in several functional areas. For example, a city health officer can call upon the more extensive laboratory facilities of a state public health department to assist him in identifying diseases or other public health hazards. Another example is that of the state police agencies making available to local law enforcement agencies the information commonly maintained in state central criminal information files. State-local relationships, however, often exceed technical aid or information reciprocity.

These more formal relationships can be divided into four categories.[1] In the first are those resulting from the delegation of a function by a state administrative department to a local agency department, subject to the acceptance of state policies and review. A state agriculture department, for example, might designate a city health department to inspect dairies located outside the city but supplying milk to it. In the second are those relationships resulting from state inspection of local agency performance, and local enforcement of state-established standards designed to protect public health and welfare. For example, city sanitation departments enforce state rules and policies on water pollution prevention. In the third category are those relationships resulting from allocation of state money to encourage or aid certain locally performed functions, such as local school programs. In the fourth are those relationships resulting from the administrative enforcement of detailed legislative restrictions placed on the expenditure by local agencies of funds collected by the state and shared with local governments. An outstanding example of this is the administration of state-collected, locally shared gasoline taxes. State legislation establishes detailed controls on local expenditure of these funds, so that local agencies are required to make specific reports and submit project-authorization requests to the state highway department.

The state's authority can extend to the intervention by state law enforcement officials in areas where local law enforcement breaks down. In other cases, the local administration of such functions as public health and education can be set aside and state administration substituted. Patterns of state-local relations differ in different sections of the country, but the fact that local agencies are essentially political subdivisions of the state establishes a relationship in which the state is legally superior. It must be recognized, of course, that local agencies can have a major effect on state policies through the political process.

There are also many relationships among local units in the same geographic area. State legislation generally permits and often encourages cooperative arrangements between local agencies. Such arrangements recognize that many of the problems caused by rapid urban growth extend beyond the boundaries of a single jurisdiction, and consequently require solutions that single agencies cannot provide alone. For example, single

---

[1] From Winston W. Crouch, *Intergovernmental Relations,* Haynes Foundation, Los Angeles, Calif., 1954, pp. 2-3.

agencies are often unable to handle demands on sewer, water, and transportation systems caused by development outside the area that the facilities were originally designed to serve. Recreation, law enforcement, and land use planning are further examples of services with broad geographic impact. Many cities have contracts or agreements with the county in which they are located whereby the county performs certain functions for the city. In California, for example, the assessment and collection of property taxes and the provision of public health services, which can legally be performed by individual cities, are usually assigned by the cities to the county government by agreement. Cities also contract with each other for services, often by means of joint-powers agreements. Informal cooperation between functional departments in different units of government is also frequent, particularly by the police, utility, fire, and public works agencies, which often cooperate in establishing informal levels of service. Another cooperative device for urban service has been consolidation of functions in which one government agency provides a functional service such as public health, traffic control, or sewage on a contractual basis to other governmental units in the area.

Expansion of the relationships among local agencies of government has been strongly motivated by urban metropolitan growth, particularly since World War II. In a few cases, federated systems have evolved whereby the local units elect representatives to a more comprehensive urban government for the metropolitan area. Nearly all cooperative arrangements, however, preserve the identity of the individual local units.

Although the units of local government are distinct organizational entities, it should be remembered that many of them overlap in territorial jurisdiction. Cities are within counties, and districts of all types overlap cities, counties, and one another. This patchwork of overlapping geographic responsibilities is a major characteristic of local government.

The major relevance of these intergovernmental relationships to data system design lies in the fact that many governments are concerned with the same data. This fact, as we shall see in Chapter 4, is a dominant factor in designing long-range systems to serve state and local governments.

General Characteristics

In addition to understanding the functions, structures, and mutual relationships of state and local governments, it is important to appreciate certain other significant characteristics of these agencies. These characteristics are particularly relevant to the design of data systems, although their importance exceeds this one consideration.

First, *there is great variety in the size of state and local units*. For example, cities range in population from a few hundred to several million people, but more than half of them have fewer than 2500. Local agency annual budgets similarly range from several thousand dollars for some districts to many millions for large counties, cities, and districts. This variety in size is reflected in operating policies and in the data systems these units have developed. Since larger units deal with more data, they ordinarily have been the first to mechanize their data systems. Smaller governmental units have traditionally believed their data volume too small to make automatic equipment economically feasible.

Second, *local units have a strong tradition of autonomy and home rule.* The determination of local officials to operate their own programs in their own way has a long history in American local government. Many battles have been fought between city hall and the state capitol over control of local unit operations. During the early part of the century, cities and counties were successful in obtaining considerable autonomy of operation. However, to a greater extent, local officials have become willing to accept financial assistance from state and Federal governments even though there may be strings attached affecting the character and administration of the services they provide. Despite this erosion, the tradition of home rule remains strong, especially in cities and counties.

Third, *there is a long-standing division in American state and local governments between urban and rural interests.* As the urban areas have grown, the rural areas have declined and lost some of their predominance; however, since many state legislatures are still dominated by representatives from rural areas, legislation designed to meet the problems of urban growth is often difficult to pass if rural interests feel their welfare would be endangered. The urban-rural split is accompanied in some states by regional interests, where north and south or east and west have different interests which collide in the state legislature.

Fourth, *the presence in most state and local governments of a large number of directly elected officials and functional diversity has led to strong departmental autonomy apart from the executive control of the governor, mayor, or other chief administrative official.* The presence of many elected officials is in the American tradition of checks and balances, and is designed to disperse power, on the theory that power corrupts and, consequently, should not be placed into too few hands. Strong departmental independence is often reinforced by the presence of administrative boards and commissions interposed between the chief executive and the department heads he appoints. Although the strong functional department orientation is often tempered by enlightened administrators with broad viewpoints, sometimes absurd parochialism can be found. For example, an elected county recorder may claim that he has "a mandate from the people" to keep his files in a particularly archaic way. Since he answers to no one but the electorate, it is difficult without his assent to improve a system over which he has almost absolute authority. Another species of independence is the vertical allegiance often found among functional specialists in the same line of work. Public health and police officials, for example, all the way from the tiny township up to the state department, often form reciprocal loyalties that are even stronger than the loyalties of the departments to their parent governmental jurisdiction (city, county, or state). Intergovernmental data systems therefore have typically developed on a functional, rather than on a jurisdictional, basis.

Fifth, *a corollary to strong departmental independence is the frequently occurring weakness of central executive authority in state and local governments.* This is particularly true in county and some state governments. School districts, many special districts, and cities with strong mayors or city managers and states with strong governors, often have enhanced the power of the central executive; but, even so, this officer is almost universally less powerful than his counterpart in a business organization. Such a phenomenon is significant for data system design because procedural integration among departments is more difficult if there is no "strong boss" to provide central leadership.

Sixth, *because state and local governments are public entities, they are governed by laws, and the influence of legislative control is very strong.* Detailed prescriptive public laws govern almost every phase of state and local government and often foster considerable procedural rigidity in data systems. Once passed, public laws become policies which must be followed by administrative departments even though they may prescribe a procedure or method that proves in practice to be cumbersome and unworkable. Nothing can be changed without passing another law modifying the original one and generally also spelling out in great detail the who, what, when, where, and how of each administrative step. On the other side of the coin, however, state laws can promote uniformity in administrative practice and thus facilitate intergovernmental and interfunctional cooperation. Of course, there is no reason why good administrative procedure as well as poor cannot be written into public law.

TRENDS AND PROSPECTS

Since this study is primarily directed toward development of data systems for the future, let us consider some of the trends and prospects in state and local government organizations and functions that will affect the design of such systems.

First, *population will increase, particularly in urban areas.* Census statistics show that 64 per cent of the nation's population lived in urban areas in 1950, and 70 per cent in 1960. The population in standard metropolitan statistical areas also increased from 87,600,000 (58 per cent) to 112,900,000 (63 per cent) and the number of these areas from 168 to 212 during the period from 1950 to 1960. The words "growth" and "urban," therefore, epitomize the future environment with which governments must plan to deal.

Second, *state and local government services will expand, probably faster than population growth*. Since denser urban populations demand more of the services that state and local governments provide, there is little likelihood of a decline or delay in the growth of these functions and services.

Third, *within the organization of state and local government agencies, the leadership and control of the central executive officer will increase, and consequently the independence of functional departments will decrease*. The majority of government reorganization proposals in recent years has included plans for strengthening the central executive; actions taken by governmental units, although not going so far as many of the proposals recommend, have strengthened the position of governors, mayors, city managers, and other central administrative officials. The effects for governmental units will include more integration across departments, procedural standardization, reduction in the number and traditional independence of separate functional departments, and increased central financial and operational control. The executive budget will continue to be a major instrument for expanded central executive control.

Fourth, *there will be continued expansion in intergovernmental relationships*. In the state-local sphere, procedures in intergovernmental dealings will become more standardized under leadership of the state government. Rule-making and standard-setting are already common means for state supervision of local functions. They are particularly well developed in public welfare, public health, and public education, and their expansion into other functions such as law enforcement, mental health, and recreation will follow with the increase of the interdependency of urban life. In several states, the present work of standardizing the charts of accounts among cities and counties will lead to more uniformity in accounting practices. The growing role in some states of state boundary commissions to review the expansion and modification of municipal territories is a further example of increasing state interest in and review of local agency activity. A second area of related state-local relationships will be the setting of minimum levels of service by the state for the guidance of local agencies. The grant and subvention of funds by the state to its local subdivisions is often the administrative medium through which minimum levels of service are established and adherence to them is controlled. Among local agencies in the same metropolitan area, joint and cooperative arrangements will be expanded both to perform functions of area-wide concern and to achieve economies of large-scale operations.

Fifth, *some form of area government for dealing with metropolitan problems will evolve in many places.* Although the home-rule tradition of local agencies will delay the development of larger, more embracing forms of local government, the need for broader representation and more comprehensive planning and action will lead eventually to some form of metropolitan government in many urban areas. Problems of health, planning, utilities, law enforcement, sewage disposal, and public transportation transcend the sole concern of the local governmental unit acting in isolation. Scores of tiny governmental jurisdictions cannot continue to operate independently. As rural areas become urban, traditional government structures also must change. Urban service districts and multipurpose metropolitan districts, authorized in recent legislative sessions around the country, are current efforts to ameliorate the problems of urban growth while retaining a degree of home rule for local agencies.

Although most likely metropolitan area governments with some comprehensive responsibilities will evolve eventually, city, county, and district units of government will generally continue to exist. Integration of specific functions seems likely, for performance either by a metropolitan area government itself or by one of the several cities, counties, or districts within the metropolitan area on behalf of many governmental units. Public health, transportation, water supply, land use planning, and regional recreation are among the functions frequently identified as those which should be integrated for performance by a single government agency for an entire metropolitan area. Already, in some sections of the country, counties are contracting with cities for the performance by the county of common municipal services within city boundaries.

The particular form that metropolitan government or functional integration takes does not appear to be critical, since we can certainly assume that these methods of achieving intergovernmental simplification will be used to a greater extent in the future. Laws in several states now provide that cities may contract with each other or with the county, and that counties may contract with each other and the cities, to perform services for each other in the most expeditious way. Since the state, of course, can perform any of the functions of its political subdivisions, the legal framework for continued functional integration, consolidation, and simplification is generally available.

Sixth, *certain functions will expand rapidly as state and local governments respond to demands for public services.* In particular, the following functions promise to grow faster than the average rate of growth for all functions together: urban planning, redevelopment and renewal, education, vocational licensing, public welfare, culture and recreation, and mental health. It is significant that most of these functions use increasing volumes of data in their activities.

Seventh, *revenues to support these growing services will continue to be scarce, and it seems likely that the broader revenue base available to state governments will be drawn upon increasingly to provide support by means of subventions to local governments for functions performed at the local level of government.* The controls that always accompany subventions will be a force for standardization among the agencies receiving the funds.

Eighth, *the administration of state and local governments will become more professional.* Particularly since World War II, persons entering state and local governments have had extensive educational preparation. Many of the functional fields are applying more professional standards for personnel who practice welfare, education, health, planning, law enforcement, agriculture, and recreation. As administrative personnel become more professional, interest in better decision-making should increase. We believe this interest will focus more and more on improved information systems that can contribute to this objective.

These trends in state and local government functions and organization suggest the direction in which these institutions are moving. Governments change slowly, and these prospects may not all evolve together or even necessarily develop to the extent we have indicated. The trend, however, is toward expansion, integration, standardization, and professionalization.

SUMMARY

In summary, the following organizational factors are of primary importance in data system design for state and local governments:

1. The great variety of functions they perform;
2. Their diversity of type, size, and structure;
3. Their increasing interrelationships (but the continuing preservation of local units' separate identities and objectives);
4. The increasing data processing workload resulting from increasing population, expanding government services, and a growing interest in improving operations and decisions through the use of more extensive data.

CHAPTER FOUR

THE DATA

The previous chapters have discussed two major elements in a data processing system: equipment and organizations. This chapter deals with the third element: data. Data are a major ingredient in both the clerical operations and the management decisions of all organizations. They are used both individually and in combination, and are usually considered in terms of their use. Uses of data in mechanized data systems are often called applications. Applications, which consist simply of various combinations of data items, differ widely from user to user because the procedures and purposes for using data vary. Our concern is not to describe these applications or uses, but to focus on the nature of the data themselves. What specific data are used to perform state and local government functions?

Analyzing these data involves two major steps. First, the specific items of data must be identified. Second, the multitude of specific items of data must be organized into a meaningful form.

To identify these data, we visited governmental units of every type and of various sizes in several areas of the country. Although many of our examples are taken from the state of California, we found significant similarity in the data used by governmental units throughout the country. The primary method of data identification was to interview officials responsible for performing the various functions. These persons were asked what specific information they use in their functions and what additional data they would like to have available. In addition to personal interviews, extensive analysis was made of the printed forms used by these functions. This proved an effective way of identifying specific items of information because nearly all such items are collected on special forms. We also analyzed the filing methods used to store data in the various functions and studied the flow of information between governmental departments and units. In each of these methods, our focus was on specific items of data, not on aggregates of data that are commonly associated with the use of the information, such as planning data and socio-economic information.

The second phase of data analysis is organization of the multitude of specific information items into a meaningful form. State and local governments conventionally organize data around their functional uses, such as *police* data, *welfare* data, and *agricultural* data. This practice has created many parallel data systems, each limited to the requirements of the function it serves. The following are some of the results:

(a) There is extensive duplicate collection and storage of the same information items. For example, information describing land use is gathered and filed by assessors, fire departments, planning departments, utilities, and other agencies. Each agency uses the information for a different purpose, even though the information itself is essentially the same. Also, departments often maintain their own accounting records which contain the same data as are contained in the files of the central fiscal office.

(b) Information collected by one function is often unknown to other functions which could use it if they were aware of its availability and if it were in a form usable to them. For example, fire departments are often interested in the existence of private swimming pools in residential areas. Fire inspectors are frequently sent into the field to gather this information, which often could be extracted from other government files, such as building permits or assessor records.

(c) Because of jurisdictional or procedural problems, information items are not efficiently shared among functions and agencies. One large city, for example, manually maintains separate records of the ownership of all parcels of land; the county assessor keeps identical records, but because of procedural problems, the information is not available in a manner satisfactory to the city departments. A similar problem is found in such an activity as the billing of special assessment payments, in which a basic record must be kept of the ownership and address of parcels within assessment districts so that bills can be mailed periodically to the owners. Separate sets of records are typically set up for this billing process, whereas expansion of information in other files often could facilitate such processing by means of minor modifications of existing clerical machinery.

(d) Often, data that would be useful to a department are not collected at all, even though another department could easily gather these data in the course of its regular operations if it knew of the need.

These problems have resulted from the fact that each state and local government function typically has developed its own information system to fit its particular needs alone. No one has taken a comprehensive view of all the data available in one form or another within state and local governments and suggested how these data can be organized to make them more usable by all the functions that need them. The advance of EDP equipment, with its increasing capability to store and process enormous quantities of data, enables such a fresh and comprehensive analysis to be made.

We have therefore looked at state and local government data from a different perspective and have asked the question, "What basically do these data describe?" This approach leads to the organizing of data into two classifications; neither is related to the functional departments that use the data, but together they include *all* the data used by state and local governments. The first class contains data describing the *environment* in which these governments operate and for which they have some responsibility. The second class contains data relating to the *internal operations* of the government agencies themselves.

ENVIRONMENTAL DATA

In order to understand environmental data, the state and local government environment itself must be understood. It consists of three categories of objects: real property, persons, and personal property. These environmental objects are external to the government agencies themselves; that is, they are not part of or owned by government organizations. All the functions of these governments, however, are ultimately directed at affecting one or more of these objects. For example, the education function is directed toward persons, and the public works function toward real property. State and local government functions are, in effect, specified responsibilities for persons and property. Because of the diversity of agency functions, the same persons and property often fall under the jurisdiction of several governmental units and departments. For example, a person may be licensed to drive by the state, registered to vote by a county, and given welfare aid by a city. Similarly, the same parcel of real property may be taxed by the county, zoned by a city, and given fire protection by a special district. Usually several functional departments of the same governmental unit provide different services to the same persons and parcels. The significant trait of the governmental environment, therefore, is that it is *common* to many functions and agencies.

As we have seen, agencies conventionally think of data in connection with their functional use: health data, tax data, licensing data, and so forth. These uses reflect the particular responsibilities of the various agencies and departments, rather than the nature of the data. When the environmental data are analyzed, it becomes apparent that they always describe characteristics of real property, persons, or personal property, however diverse the functions for which these items of data are used. We have, therefore, categorized environmental data according to the objects they describe rather than according to their functional uses. Instead of analyzing welfare data, for example, we have identified those data about *persons* that are used to perform the welfare function. Figure 5 relates the major functions of state and local governments to the environmental information categories of primary interest to each function.

Functions	Environmental Information Categories		
	Real Property	Persons	Personal Property
1. Correction—Probation		√	
2. Culture—Recreation		√	
3. Education		√	
4. Natural Resources	√		
5. Protection	√	√	√
6. Public Health	√	√	
7. Public Welfare and Security		√	
8. Public Works	√		
9. Regulation and Licensing	√	√	√
10. Sanitation	√		
11. General Government	√	√	√
12. Proprietary	√	√	

Fig. 5. State and local government functions related to environmental information categories

On the left of this figure the twelve basic state and local government functions are identified. Within these functions there are subfunctions, activities, and subactivities down to several levels of detail. These functions are executed by different types and agencies of government, and both types and agencies differ from state to state. The nature of the functions, however, and the data that are used to perform them are remarkably similar across jurisdictional lines. Because of the relative autonomy of proprietary functions, they have been included in this study only to the extent that they generate or use data that are of interest to other government activities. Having categorized environmental data around the objects they describe, let us examine the nature of each category and the items of information within it.

Real Property Data

Real property information includes all data that describe the characteristics of land and what is on it. The characteristics of real property are particularly important to state and local governments because land is a primary natural resource that is fixed in location and limited in area. Since every event of concern to state and local governments occurs on land, the demand for many government services is generated by the condition of or activities on real property. Because of this fact, many government facilities and services are allocated on the basis of information describing real property conditions and characteristics.

For example, parks, schools, libraries, and roads are placed on land in relationship to the need for them in a given area. Measures of need may include such data as the density and age of the population or the number of registered cars in that area. Field personnel for such diverse activities as alcoholic beverage control, building inspection, police, and public welfare are assigned on the basis of data relating the functions of their agencies to some characteristic of real property—such as its use, its condition, or its occupants. In addition to allocating resources on the basis of real property information, governments perform certain specific functions relating to land and what is on it. Table 4 presents some of these functions and some of the typical government agencies concerned.

TABLE 4

SELECTED GOVERNMENTAL FUNCTIONS RELATING TO REAL PROPERTY

Function	*Agency*
Custody of records of legal title to property and encumbrances thereon	Recorder
Protection of property	Police
	Fire
	Flood control
Regulation of property development and use	Structural regulation
	Planning-zoning
	Urban renewal
	Air pollution
Provision of transportation routes across land	Roads
Removal of sewage and other wastes from property	Sanitation
Assessment of property values, levying and collection of taxes	Assessor
	Auditor
	Tax collector

Organizationally, most of these functions relating to real property are with agencies of local, rather than state, government. Similarly, almost all functions performed by special districts are primarily concerned with real property.

Not all functions and agencies collect or use all of the same data describing real property. On the other hand, certain basic information is necessary to nearly every function that uses any data. Take as an example, the real property information relating to the hypothetical characteristics of a parcel of land occupied by a drugstore:

Data	*User*
(1) The fact that this is a commercial building on a particular parcel, at a specific address, owned by a certain person, is of interest to the	Assessor
(2) Item (1), plus the fact that this building is used as a drugstore, is of interest to the	Business license office Sales tax office City planner
(3) Items (1) and (2), plus the fact that this drugstore has a liquor license, are of interest to the	Police Alcoholic beverage control office
(4) Items (1), (2), and (3), plus the fact that the store was burgled last month, are of interest to the	Police
(5) Items (1) and (2), plus the fact that there was a fire in the store in 1959, are of interest to the	Fire department
(6) Item (1), plus the fact that there is an assessment on this parcel for sewers, is of interest to the	City engineer Tax collector

Thus, certain basic information concerns several functions, although to the "total" data about each parcel of land, various functions contribute special items of interest primarily to themselves.

Items of Real Property Data. In this section we shall identify typical items of information that describe characteristics of real property. These information items, listed in Table 5, are presently being gathered and used by state and local government agencies for many functions. No function is interested in all the data, but several are concerned with an increasing proportion of them. Not all the items are applicable to or available for every parcel of land. Some items, on the other hand, are used to describe all parcels, although many of the items have not traditionally been thought of as relating to real property. The group of information items describing a particular parcel form the "record" for that parcel.

A parcel record contains information describing (1) the location of the parcel of land, both geographically and in relation to political jurisdictions affecting it; (2) the land itself and the structures upon, under, and adjacent to it; and (3) the occupants and owners of the parcel.

Data concerning public rights of way form a subcategory of real property information, which is presented separately in Table 5 as a "street section" record.

TABLE 5

REAL PROPERTY INFORMATION ITEMS [a]

PARCEL RECORD

Locational Information

1. Parcel number
2. Parcel address(es)
3. Legal description
4. Grid coordinates
5. Street section reference
   a. Side of street on which parcel lies
6. Parcel numbers of adjacent parcels
7. Political and administrative jurisdictions of all types
   a. county
   b. city
   c. township
   d. borough
   e. special district(s)
   f. school district(s)
   g. judicial district(s)
   h. voting precinct
   i. electoral district(s)—e.g., councilmanic, assembly, congressional
   j. school attendance area
   k. department administrative district or service area—police, public works, health, utility, welfare, employment security
   l. postal zone
   m. improvement or assessment district
   n. tax code area
   o. "community" or unincorporated area
   p. economic area
   q. marketing area
   r. hydrologic area
   s. fire zone or district
   t. traffic zone
   u. census tract
   v. census block and/or enumeration district

8. Physical block
9. Lot position (key, reverse, corner)
10. Maps on which parcel mapped

Land and Structural Characteristics

11. Parcel size
12. Zoning
    a. zone variance
    b. exception(s)
    c. special use permit
    d. conditional use permit
    e. nonconforming use (expiration date)
13. Master plan category and plans affecting parcel
14. Land uses, including "activities on premises"
15. Assessed value
    a. land, year assessed
    b. improvements, year assessed
    c. trees and vines, year assessed
    d. personal property at this parcel
16. Exemptions
17. Taxable value
18. Tax delinquency
19. Liens, assessments, and encumbrances
20. Deed restrictions
21. Easements
22. Water and/or mineral rights
23. Topographic characteristics
24. Drainage characteristics
25. Soil type
26. Productivity data
27. Extractive data
28. Fish and wildlife data
29. Date of last sale of parcel
30. Price at last sale of parcel
31. Rental price
32. Building characteristics
    a. number of separate buildings
    b. floor area of building(s)
    c. portion of parcel covered by building(s)
    d. setback of building(s)
    e. frontage and depth of building(s)
    f. height of building(s)
    g. number of stories in building(s)
    h. number of rooms in building(s)
    i. existence of basement(s)

      j. number of dwelling units in building(s)

      k. type and class of building construction

      l. cost of building construction

      m. year building(s) built

      n. condition of building(s)

      o. number and character of licenses and permits issued by all agencies pertaining to the structure on this parcel

33. Utilities connected
34. Waste disposal facilities
35. Presence of civil defense facility-shelter, first-aid station
36. Presence of special establishments
37. Presence of swimming pool
38. Police information

      a. crime—type, date, time, case number

      b. incident—type, date, time, case number

39. Fire information

      a. fires at this parcel—kind, date, loss

      b. fire alarm responses to this parcel—date, type (for example, false)

      c. fire prevention inspection record

         (1) date of last inspection

         (2) violations noted

         (3) special hazards identified—flammable liquids, acids, explosives, incinerator

      d. rooms certified for maximum number of occupants

      e. presence of automatic fire sprinklers, standpipes, extinguishers

      f. presence of fire walls

      g. rescue/ambulance responses to this parcel

      h. distance from parcel to nearest fire hydrant and fire alarm box

40. Public health information

      a. health hazard conditions at this parcel

      b. diseases reported at this parcel

      c. health permits (for example, food-vending establishment)

      d. inspection records (see 39c.)

41. Automobiles registered at this parcel
42. Subsurface structures and improvements
43. Neighborhood characteristics
44. Proximity to special facilities
45. Personal property at parcel

Owner-Occupant Characteristics

46. Owner's name and mailing address
47. Occupant's name(s)
48. Occupancy group
49. Vacancy information as applicable
50. Number and kind of licenses and permits of all kinds granted to occupants

51. Residential occupant characteristics
    a. number of occupants
    b. number of households
    c. number of occupants per room
    d. race of occupants
    e. sex of occupants   .
    f. age of occupants—month and year born
    g. education of occupants—years of school completed
    h. family income class
    i. voters' registration of occupants
    j. occupations of occupants
    k. major industrial groups in which occupants are employed
    l. employment status
    m. place of work
    n. means of transportation to work
    o. tenure of household head
        (1) previous address(es)
    p. occupants rent or own?
    q. occupants receiving public welfare services or assistance?
        (1) type or category of aid received
    r. occupants with criminal or correction records
    s. children in school
    t. birth-death data
52. Commercial/industrial occupant characteristics
    a. type of business(es)
    b. parcel number(s) of other parcels comprising store or plant site
    c. number of employees
    d. employee places of residence
    e. means of transportation used in getting to work
    f. off-street parking spaces provided
    g. labor force data
    h. retail sales
    i. business failures at parcel

STREET-SECTION RECORD

1. Section number
2. Section name
3. Section class (local, collector, arterial, freeway, etc.)
4. Section status
5. Section direction
6. Section limits
7. Section length
8. Intersecting sections
9. Intersection code

10. Jurisdiction code(s)
11. Section width
12. Street width
13. Section surface type
14. Section surface condition
15. Grade
16. Alignment
17. Drainage conditions
18. Traffic volume data
19. Parking space data
20. Presence of parking meters
21. Presence of curbs
22. Presence of sidewalks
23. Presence of street lights
24. Presence of sewers
25. Presence of storm drains
26. Presence of street trees
27. Presence of utility facilities
28. Presence of structures (grade crossings, bridge, tunnel)
29. Presence of traffic signals, stop signs, and other traffic control devices
30. Public transportation facilities
31. Traffic accident data—day, time, type of accidents
32. Street and curb markings
33. Speed limits
34. Fire alarm boxes
35. Plans affecting section
36. Deficiencies
37. Parcel numbers of parcels adjacent to street section

ᵃ See Appendix A for definitions and descriptions of these items of data.

Although the items in Table 5 are grouped into a comprehensive record describing a parcel or street section, it should be remembered that no such file exists in state and local governments today. This listing is a composite of real property-oriented data from the files of many agencies and functions. As such, it reveals the range of data normally gathered by state and local governments that can be organized into the real property category.

Even though the list does not contain every item of data about real property that is of interest to state and local governments, it includes the vast majority of those in which there is common interest. Other information can often be obtained by processing together these basic items of data. For example, property taxes are determined by multiplying taxable value by the rate applicable to the "tax code area." Additional items reflecting events or conditions at particular parcels can easily be added to the record.

Person Data

As we turn to the second category of environmental information—persons—two major differences from information about real property become apparent. First, persons—both human beings and fictitious persons such as corporations—are not fixed in location. In fact, mobility is one of their most significant characteristics. Second, government functions concerned with persons generally keep data only on those persons with whom they have special concern, such as law violators, licensees, institution inmates, and students. Whereas certain basic data about every parcel of real property are almost universally existent in the form of assessment records, no comprehensive file exists anywhere on every person.

These two major differences from the characteristics of real property invite us to consider the objectives and purposes which state and local government agencies have with respect to persons. In most of the following remarks, "persons" refers to people, although the reader can easily relate many of the comments to fictitious persons as well.

As shown in Fig. 5, several of the twelve major functions performed by state and local governments are primarily concerned with persons; this concern is expressed in three major responsibilities or activities: (1) to regulate, (2) to provide service, and (3) to maintain legal records. For example, the correction-probation function involves regulation of persons on parole and probation. Recreation, education, and public assistance are services, whereas licensing is essentially a regulatory activity. Legal records consist of such instruments as birth, death, and marriage certificates and court documents. Some government functions and many government agencies discharge more than one of these basic responsibilities.

Functions such as law enforcement, education, and welfare have a specific clientele of individuals, each of whom is of specific concern to governmental units by name. Other functions provide service or regulation to a broad aggregate of persons whose individual identities are of little concern. This is especially true in the culture-recreation functions and in some aspects of public protection and health. Primarily, however, data about persons concern individual people, and aggregates are of interest mainly for planning, research, and statistical analysis.

Information about persons in the files of state and local governments falls into two broad groups. First are items of personal identification. These items are both variable, such as weight, address, and marital status, and constant, such as sex, race, fingerprint classification, date born, and Social Security number. The second broad group of information items describes the status of a specific person with respect to certain government functions. Although all governmental units, in order to maintain any records on specific persons, need certain similar identity data, status data differ greatly between state and local government functions.

These differences in status data are based primarily on the different clientele of the various functions and on the service or regulation they provide. Thus, for example, the number and expiration date of a vocational license to practice nursing is of specific concern to the state department that regulates professional and vocational licensing. This information is of no interest, however, to the department of corrections if the licensee has never been within its jurisdiction. In order for either the department of professional and vocational standards or the department of corrections to maintain records on *any* persons who are of interest to them, however, certain identity data about such persons must be recorded. When several functions or organizations are interested in the same person, identity and certain status data are duplicated under conventional information systems. For example, much of the same information about a particular person is gathered by both employment and welfare agencies.

Information Items Describing Persons. This section identifies typical items of information that describe persons. These items, given in Table 6, are currently being gathered and used by many state and local government agencies in performing a multitude of functions. Not all are applicable to, or available for, every person, but some are used to describe every person about whom any government agency keeps records. As listed, the items represent a comprehensive record of information about a person.

The items are of two classes: (1) those identifying the person and (2) those describing the status of the person with respect to the functions of one or more government agencies. These items reflect both current and historical information about the person involved.

TABLE 6

PERSON INFORMATION ITEMS [a]

I. *IDENTITY DATA*

    1. Name
    2. Social Security number
    3. Sex
    4. Date of birth
    5. Place of birth
    6. Date of death
    7. Place of death
    8. Race/descent
    9. Religion

10. Current address
    a. date moved to current address
    b. permanent address
11. Previous address(es)
12. Date came to state
13. Date came to county
14. Height
15. Weight
16. Color eyes
17. Color hair
18. Complexion of skin
19. Marks and scars
20. Physical handicaps
21. Blood type
22. Marital status
    a. date and place of marriage(s)
    b. name of spouse
    c. name(s) of former spouse(s)
    d. data describing any divorce decrees
23. Citizenship
24. Fingerprint classification
25. Military service
    a. period of service
    b. branch of service
    c. type of discharge
    d. service serial number
26. Selective Service number
27. Parents' names and Social Security numbers
28. Children's names and Social Security numbers
29. Siblings' names and Social Security numbers

II. STATUS DATA

A. Voters' Registration Status

30. Party
31. Precinct
32. Elections in which vote cast

B. Licenses and Permits

33. Type of license or permit
34. Number
35. Date issued
36. Expiration date (if any)
37. Issuing agency
38. Special conditions

C. Law Enforcement Data

    39. Outstanding warrants
       a. issuing court
       b. law enforcement agency involved
       c. offense charged
       d. date of warrant
       e. warrant number
    40. Offense(s) record
       a. type of offense
       b. date of offense
       c. case or record number
       d. disposition
       e. law enforcement agency or agencies
    41. Ex-convict registration number
       a. registration date
       b. law enforcement agency involved
    42. Missing persons
       a. date reported missing
       b. location last known
       c. law enforcement agency involved

D. Court Actions

    43. Plaintiff and defendant
    44. Court
    45. Case number
    46. Type of action
    47. Date
    48. Disposition

E. Probation/Parole Data

    49. Probation or parole number
    50. Court and case number
    51. Probation or parole agency
    52. Offense (or delinquent act)
    53. Date
    54. Term of probation or parole
    55. Special conditions

F. Employment Data

    56. Current employer
    57. Employer number
    58. Employer address
    59. Date employed
    60. Employer Standard Industrial Classification Code
    61. Previous employers

62. Occupation of person
63. Unemployment date
64. Earnings within the past year
65. Payments received

G. Confinement Data

66. Type of confinement
67. Period of confinement
68. Place of confinement
69. Reason for confinement
70. Commitment authorization
71. Treatment data
72. Confinement escapes

H. Welfare Data

73. County case number
74. State case number
75. Category of aid received
76. Amount of aid received
77. Periods during which aid received
78. Basis for aid

I. Health Data

79. Physical deficiencies
80. Reportable diseases
81. Special conditions
82. Immunization and X-ray data

J. Educational Data

83. Schools attended
84. Periods of attendance
85. Courses completed
86. Degrees granted
87. Intelligence or achievement test results

K. Miscellaneous Data

88. Income tax bureau number
    a. year(s) return filed
    b. income tax group
    c. number and name(s) of dependents claimed
89. Parcel numbers of real property
90. Registration numbers of personal property
91. Registration numbers of firms in which person is involved
92. Organization memberships
93. Government agencies with further information

a See Appendix A for definitions and descriptions of these items of data.

In addition to such information about people, there are data describing fictitious persons, mainly corporations and other business enterprises. Such data generally include the following items: business name, principal owners or corporate officers, business address, mailing address, political jurisdiction, type of organization (individual, corporation, partnership), nature of business, number of employees, state corporation number, and any business license numbers. Typically, these data are in separate departmental files for such functions as licensing, unemployment insurance, income tax, sales tax, industrial safety, and "doing-business-as" or corporate registration. Organization of the information around the firm described follows the same logic as that which applies to information concerning individual persons.

Obviously, Table 6 does not list every item of data about persons in the files of state and local governmental units, but it comprehensively describes the *kind* of items that logically could make up a basic record concerning an individual person. Additional items could easily be included within the record.

Personal Property Data

The final category of environmental data relates to personal property, legally defined as "all property except real property." Despite the comprehensiveness suggested by this definition, the interest of governments in personal property is largely restricted to taxation and regulation. Taxation applies to a broad class of personal property articles; regulation to a narrow class.

Personal property is affected by taxation at the time of sale and periodically in relation to ownership. We are not concerned with sales tax in this study because no information describing the individual items sold is transmitted to the government by the retailer. Only aggregate sales by broad category are reported. The term "property tax" generally refers, as it does here, to the annual levy assessed against the value of property. The specific items of information involved in the assessment and collection of personal property taxes are discussed below.

Whereas taxation applies to almost all articles of personal property, regulation applies to very few. In some classes of personal property, notably automobiles, both taxation and regulation are often accomplished in the process of licensing. The purpose of regulation is to protect the public health, welfare, or safety from the dangerous or improper use of personal property items.

Classes of Personal Property. Personal property about which state and local governments are concerned can be divided into two major classes: registered and nonregistered.

Registered personal property includes
Vehicles
Automobiles, trucks, trailers, buses, ambulances
Motorcycles
Bicycles
Airplanes
Boats
House trailers
Private railroad cars
Elevators
Firearms
Weighing and measuring devices
Dogs

Nonregistered personal property includes

Commercial personal property
Machinery and equipment
Office equipment
Trade equipment
Merchandise/inventory
Cash
Trade fixtures
Solvent credits
Noncommercial personal property
Household furnishings

A serial number of some kind is generally assigned to each registered article of property within the class. The aim of registration is primarily to facilitate regulation. For example, each firearm is separately registered at the time of sale and each dog has a separate license number. Nonregistered property is of concern to governments primarily for taxation purposes. Information about it is usually in the form of an aggregate value figure for each of the classes above rather than a tally or description of the individual articles within each class, such as light fixtures or office desks. Generally, personal property subject to assessment and taxation is not enumerated or registered for this purpose. Instead, a gross value figure for all personal property owned by a person at a given location is recorded. It is generally the responsibility of the property owner annually to declare his property and its value, and from this basic source, together with field observation of the property itself, the assessor arrives at a value figure. Regulation of nonregistered property occurs in the case of factory equipment whose operation involves safety hazards.

Items of Information. Information items describing personal property are designed to answer three questions: What is it?—identity and description; Where is it?—location; and, To whom does it belong?—ownership.

For classes of registered personal property, the information items relating to the identity of the property are usually more extensive than for non-registered property. For example, typical items of information for motor vehicles in California are as follows:

1. License number and type
2. Name of owner
3. Address of owner, including city and county
4. Identification or engine number
5. Make
6. Body type
7. Model
8. Cylinders
9. Date first sold
10. Year of model
11. Serial number
12. Motive power
13. Axles
14. Unladen weight
15. Wheel base
16. Name of legal owner or lien holder, including his address
17. Date first operated in California
18. Whether vehicle is new or used
19. Whether the vehicle is registered in another state or county
20. Whether vehicle is to be used for transportation of persons or property for hire (if used for hire, the Board of Equalization permit number)

Most of these items identify the vehicle and its owner; a few refer to its use. Information dealing with other registered vehicles is similar. In the case of firearms, weighing and measuring devices, and dogs, data items relating to the location of the property and to its ownership are the most significant.

Location and ownership are the most important features of non-registered personal property, which is of interest primarily for taxation because the major descriptive identity data relate to aggregates of value. Nature of equipment, location, and ownership are also the prime concern in cases of equipment subject to safety regulation.

System Considerations. In contrast to data about persons and real property where multiple use is made of the same items of information by several agencies and functions of government, information about each class of personal property generally seems to be used only by the single agency responsible for collecting it. Consequently, there would be no benefit in organizing all types of personal property information into a single file. Rather, an individual file for each class of personal property seems appropriate, with each file under the jurisdiction of the agency primarily responsible for the regulation or taxation involved. Many states have already followed this practice for motor vehicles and firearms, maintaining state-wide central files for each of these classes. Any authorized agency or person may interrogate these central files.

This does not mean that the filing and communications aspects of these systems could not be improved, but that the improvements would be primarily technical rather than conceptual. The existing concept of maintaining files of data about personal property as an adjunct of the particular function appears sound.

The *ownership* and *location* of personal property listed in these separate files could be appropriately noted in the person and/or real property files described in earlier sections. Such files would contain only the basic personal property description and a cross reference to the appropriate personal property file which contains the complete data. All files would be updated by automatic byproduct notification from the agencies concerned.

For example, the presence of a scale or a registered car at a particular address is a characteristic of the parcel involved and, therefore, forms an item of data in the real property record about the parcel. Data describing the detailed characteristics of the scale or car would be maintained exclusively by the functional department concerned. Likewise, this is true of aggregate personal property of concern to assessors.

Occasionally, the basic description of the personal property article, together with its ownership and location, are its only recorded data. With respect to household furnishings, for example, all necessary data can be recorded in the person and/or real property files, and no separate personal property file is necessary.

Conclusion. The basic difference between personal property on the one hand, and persons and real property on the other, is that few functions are interested in the former, whereas many are interested in the latter. This difference suggests that there should be greater conceptual changes in the handling of information describing persons and real property. Technological advances in data handling equipment, however, will apply to handling environmental information in all three categories.

INTERNAL DATA

The second major classification of data used by state and local governments relates to the internal operations of the agencies themselves. Internal data pertain to the resources actually owned or controlled by government agencies and used by them in performing their functions. These resources consist of dollars, employees, equipment, and facilities. Internal data are used primarily to account for these resources and to describe the activities in which they are used.

Some typical uses of data on internal resources are appropriation accounting, payroll, and inventory records for equipment and facilities. These uses deal primarily with the problem of accounting for government-owned and controlled resources. Data describing activities in which these resources are used include, for example, work unit statistics, performance ratings, and work standards.

Each state and local governmental unit has its own resources: its own dollars, employees, equipment, and facilities. Data concerning the resources and operations of a particular agency are generally of interest only to that agency. Summary statistics are occasionally reported to other agencies, but these are a byproduct rather than an operating use of the data. Because each agency is independently concerned with its own internal data, systems to handle such data should be designed to fit the specific operational requirements of the agency concerned. These requirements will vary widely with differences in agency character, size, and organizational structure. Efforts are under way to standardize accounting procedures among agencies, and the development of uniform procedures for handling internal data of similar agencies is highly worthwhile. Such procedures, however, almost always deal with data that are of unique operating interest to a single agency.

Systems for handling environmental data, on the other hand, must be designed in recognition of the fact that many agencies deal with the same environment and, therefore, have a common interest in many of the same data. We recognize, of course, that both internal and environmental data are frequently used together. For example, when a license or permit is issued, some of the information handled is of the environmental type—pertaining to the licensee—whereas the data dealing with revenue obtained from the issuance of the license is used for applications that are solely internal to the licensing agency. The design of systems for dealing with these two classes of data must, however, begin with a recognition of the fundamental difference between the classes. Because internal data are of interest to a single agency and environmental data are of interest to many agencies, we shall concentrate on environmental data in the remainder of this study.

Improvements in systems for handling the internal data of individual agencies are possible, and in Appendix B we suggest some principles that agencies should follow in the design of such systems. We believe, however, that more significant benefits can be achieved by improving systems for handling data describing the environment which many state and local governments share in common.

CHAPTER FIVE

THE UNIFIED INFORMATION SYSTEM:
ORGANIZATION

INTRODUCTION

Long-range plans for state and local government data systems must take the following facts into account:

1. The capability of data handling equipment is already large and is expanding rapidly (Chapter 2).

2. The state and local governments within a particular state, although diverse in organization and function, form a group of kindred public institutions. While each enjoys substantial autonomy, their interrelationships and interdependencies are likely to expand (Chapter 3).

3. State and local governments use data for a great variety of purposes, but many of these data describe an environment of persons and property that is common to many agencies and departments (Chapter 4).

For these reasons, we strongly urge that state and local governments should move toward a long-range goal of participating on a state-wide basis in a Unified Information System. Each of these three words is significant. *System* means that environmental data used by the state, counties, townships, cities, and special districts are related by specific procedures that are cooperative and comprehensive. *Information* restricts the objectives and operations of this system to items of data alone; no changes are demanded in the functions, basic organizational structure, or management responsibility of governmental units. *Unified* describes the grouping of the data and the blend of data processing activities into a combination of centralization and decentralization which is appropriate to the organization and functions of state and local governments.

The Unified Information System, designed for the 1970's, has two major objectives: (1) to reduce duplication in the collection, storage, and processing of data used by state and local governments; and (2) to increase the accessibility and usefulness of these data. In furthering these objectives, the System is based on and incorporates foreseeable advances in EDP technology.

We recognize that such a state-wide, intergovernmental system cannot be achieved either immediately or in a single step. Rather, the various governmental units would, and should, first develop information systems that satisfy their individual needs. These systems should employ existing data processing equipment and be designed to fit logically into the Unified Information System which future EDP capability will make possible. Chapter 8 discusses the design of such individual systems. Our purpose here is to outline a system for the 1970's that will provide a desirable goal for state and local governments to consider.

Figure 6 schematically illustrates the broad concept of the Unified Information System, showing an information system network comprising governmental units, their constituent departments, and an Information Center. Although the figure depicts only one unit, four departments, and one Center, an operating state-wide system could encompass hundreds of the first, thousands of the second, and several of the third. In essence, the

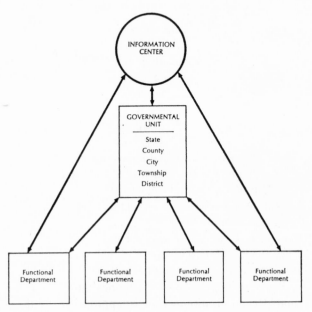

Fig. 6.   Unified Information System: over-all concept
showing flow of data

Unified Information System provides an Information Center to store and process data that are gathered and used by state and local governments within a particular state. The System is designed primarily to enable environmental data to be efficiently organized into records about the persons or property they describe. These data would be gathered in the regular operations of government agencies and transmitted to the Information Center via communication channels, often the conventional telephone network. Similarly, agencies could obtain from the Center either raw or processed data. The System does not require the collection of any new data and is entirely independent of the purposes or procedures for which the data are used. It simply provides a technological facility to file these data and to process them according to the instructions of participating agencies. Therefore, it does not alter the present relationships between any citizen and the government or those between government agencies.

Although widespread participation in the System by governmental units is necessary to realize most of its benefits, participation of all agencies within a state would not be mandatory. Over-all costs and benefits would be the primary factors determining agency participation. The following sections of this chapter discuss the role of the Information Center and the issue of centralization. Chapter 6 discusses the major activities of the System, and Chapter 7, its estimated costs and the benefits it would yield. In describing the Unified Information System, we have aimed at the conceptual, rather than the procedural, level; the what, not the how. Procedures, we believe, are best developed by operating government personnel, especially since they will likely differ substantially from state to state. The concept of the Unified Information System is both desirable and applicable within all states.

THE INFORMATION CENTER

In the Unified Information System, the one organization new to state and local governments is the Information Center. As an organization, the Center may be placed at more than one physical location and will consist of a computer complex and the personnel to operate it. Its major functions are (1) storing data, (2) processing data according to the instructions of participating agencies, and (3) supplying data as needed. In performing these functions, which are discussed in detail in Chapter 6, the Center is more than a "service bureau" that processes client data for separate agencies. It is the central element of a comprehensive system in which all phases of data handling are related by coordinated procedures. This section discusses several aspects of Center organization and administration that are important in carrying out its major functions.

Organizational Position of the Center

We believe that the Information Center should be organizationally separate from any existing unit of government. Because it renders service to cities, counties, townships, districts, and the state, locating the Center within the organization of any one of these units could lessen its usefulness to the rest. Nevertheless, it should be a public agency, created by the collective action of these units and responsible to them. This responsibility could be enforced by a board of managers elected by the participating agencies, which would set policies for the Center's internal operation. This would be the limit of the Board's authority. It would have no power to make policy affecting the operations of the participating agencies in any way. Since the basic structure and operations of the System and the Center would be spelled out in the enabling state legislation, the Board's primary functions would be (1) to appoint an executive director to supervise the Center's day-to-day operations and (2) to establish charges for the services rendered to participating agencies.

Financial Support of the Center

We believe the Center should be supported entirely by charges for services rendered. Initial establishment of the Center could logically be financed by legislative appropriation to be repaid over a period of years. Charges to participating agencies could be based on such considerations as the number of persons and/or parcels within the jurisdiction of each agency, the number of transactions requested by the agency, and the items of information that are involved in storing these data and processing these transactions.

The cost of the Unified Information System for a particular state is discussed in Chapter 7.

Number of Center Locations

We believe that it will be technologically possible to store and process data for an entire state at one location. Files of the magnitude discussed in Chapter 6, together with the estimated numbers of transactions involved, could be handled by one computer complex. This, however, is not a requirement for the success of the Unified Information System. Instead, several separate locations would be possible, and might even be desirable for economic or organizational reasons. These locations can be linked by communication nets so that they function logically as a single Center. The number of locations in any state will depend on such considerations as the amount of storage and processing to be done by the Center (versus processing by individual governmental units), the volume of transactions to be handled by the Center, the desired utilization of equipment to be employed, and the attitude toward the vulnerability of a single center.

Much of the information transmitted to the Center could be partially preprocessed by participating agencies; other data could be processed entirely by the Center. A detailed system analysis for each agency would reveal the best combination of local and central processing for that agency—and in total, for the state-wide system.

The type of computing equipment also is relevant to the number of Center locations. Computing machines are becoming larger and faster, and, assuming full utilization, the cost per unit of work is decreasing. (Decreases in unit cost cannot be significant, however, unless the work load is large enough to keep the equipment continually operating.) Therefore, if the newest and largest equipment is selected, fewer locations would probably result. The proper size and capability of equipment would depend, of course, on the requirements for data handling in each state.

Another important factor affecting the number of Center locations is the question of vulnerability. It might be argued that it is foolhardy to store so much data on an entire state in a single location, because of the danger of either man-made or natural catastrophe. There are several ways to handle this problem. One is to disperse the physical locations of the Center so that if one location were destroyed, or became temporarily inoperable, the others could carry on. If a single location were desired, however, the vulnerability question could be solved by duplicating all transaction records and shipping them daily to a separate location for safekeeping. In addition, the Center's complete files could be duplicated periodically and stored in the same remote location. If the Center were destroyed, the files could be reconstructed by using the last duplicate files and the duplicate transactions that took place since they were prepared. This is analogous to the system now utilized by the Social Security Administration.

The exact number of Center locations within a state must, therefore, be based on several considerations. Principally, the focal and overriding point here is that the Center should be designed to facilitate data handling for all the state's governmental units, rather than to fit into any one unit's organizational structure.

Administrative Responsibilities of the Center

Confidentiality. The Information Center will have the problem of maintaining the confidentiality of information stored in its files. In some instances, confidentiality is the desire of the agency which collected the data, but usually it is required by law. Once having determined which information should have restricted access, there are several ways to ensure it.

First, it is possible to use input/output station equipment with a lock which must be key operated before the equipment can be used. The agency where the remote equipment is located would be responsible for assigning keys, and any compliance by the Center with a request for information could be presumed to be authorized because only persons with authorized access would be given keys.

Another method uses a code of predetermined characters that must be entered at the input/output station before the Center will recognize the message as authorized. Each type of information can be assigned a code that is given only to persons authorized to receive the information. The codes can be changed periodically to ensure that they are used only by authorized personnel.

In most situations it will be easier to guarantee confidentiality in the Unified Information System than it is under existing manual data systems. Electronic computers carry out programmed orders with far more rigor than do people. If a machine is "told" to give information only to persons with proper credentials (i.e., a code or a key), it will "obey."

Furthermore, the confidentiality achievable with electronic computers makes it possible to perform tasks which today are either very difficult or entirely infeasible. For example, two or more agencies (e.g., welfare and public health) may separately collect data from citizens with the stipulation that the persons' names be kept confidential. Valuable correlations can often be made between these and other sets of data if the confidentiality can be protected, for in most cases the identity of persons is irrelevant to statistical analysis. The computer is an ideal tool for such a problem because it can look at the sets of data, make the required comparisons, and correlate the data exactly as instructed—all the while keeping personal identities secret within itself. Careful aggregation techniques often can achieve the same end. These techniques are not possible in manual systems, but are entirely feasible in a computerized data system because of the speed with which data can be manipulated.

That so many data about persons should be stored in one organization may also be of concern, but actually none of the data items to be stored in the Unified Information System would be new in any sense of the word. All of them are currently gathered and stored by separate agencies. We are merely suggesting that they could be stored more efficiently. Anything now confidential would remain so, and public information would remain public. Thus, there would be no change in the availability or confidentiality of information; there would be only more convenient access, once that access had been authorized.

In summary, the Unified Information System involves no new problems of confidentiality. On the contrary, any required restriction on data access can be enforced more effectively in such a System than in present separate systems.

Computer Programming. We envision that persons employed directly by the Center will perform most of the programming for the computers at the Center. Most governmental units will not need to employ their own skilled computer programmers but will need only to specify to the Center in simple English and conventional flow charts how they wish data to be processed. Center programmers will then follow these agency instructions in writing computer programs. In addition to writing special computer programs in response to agency instructions, Center personnel could develop standard programs to process data for common applications. For example, standard computer programs for tax assessment or welfare budget computation could be developed and made available to appropriate agencies. Using a standard program would generally be less costly to an agency than developing a special program for its sole use. Of course, in every case the Center would provide a computer program for processing the data exactly as the requesting agency specified. We emphasize that the Center would simply and exclusively carry out the instructions of the participating agencies.

Standardization and Coding of Terminology. If the data stored in the Unified Information System are to have value for several agencies, their meaning must be clear. "Occupation," "Type of Offense," "Land Use," "Type of Construction," "Zone Variance"—these and all the other common data items must be given standardized meanings. This does not mean that each agency must use precisely the same terms. Rather, equivalencies must be worked out between local meanings and some standardized meaning for the same term. For example, if a county regional planning commission wants a county-wide zoning inventory, the commercial zones of all the cities in that county must be merged into standard classifications for the entire county. The cities can use any designations they desire, but each one must be given a standard classification equivalent. Once such standardization has been achieved, computer programs can make automatic conversion from one meaning to another. Furthermore, data records in the System can include codes representing both local and standardized common meanings.

Besides encouraging standardization of meaning, the Unified Information System intensifies the need for coding items of information. In a parcel record, the code "BL-7" is vastly preferable to the six-word description "business license for selling retail automobiles." This code contains exactly the same information but can be stored electronically in one-tenth the space. Codification is also a prerequisite to efficient data processing, since comparisons and computations using narrative words and phrases consume excessive computer time. Each item of information should be examined to determine its suitability for coding. (It should be noted that the computer can print out in English, as one form of output, the full narrative description from a code designation. Similarly, data can be collected in narrative form, if more convenient, provided they are coded prior to entry into the computer system.) We believe Information Center personnel should take the lead in encouraging further standardization and coding. As dicussed further in Chapter 8, this should be a cooperative effort among the Center personnel, professional associations of government personnel, and the participating agencies.

Articulation of Information Requirements. In the subsequent discussion of input to the Unified Information System, we stress the need for considering each input method and instrument as a source of data for *all* agencies in the System. Items of data to serve the needs of agencies other than the one immediately involved in observing a particular event will, therefore, often be gathered by the "event observer." Such a system for comprehensive data collection requires that the need for the data involved be comprehensively articulated. If, for example, a social worker is asked to observe and report an unfenced swimming pool for the benefit of the building and safety department, the need for this information must be made known to the social welfare department. We believe that the Information Center can provide the forum within which such information needs can be expressed. Agencies can identify the data they need, and Center personnel with comprehensive knowledge of possible input sources for those data can suggest ways of gathering the data (or extracting them from existing files). Optimum ways of collecting common data can also be worked out to minimize duplication in the data collection process.

In summary, the Center can act as a clearing house for improving all phases of the total information process, as well as for storing and processing data on persons and real property.

Additional Center Services. The Information Center would also be able to store and process both specialized environmental data and internal data for participating agencies on a service bureau basis. Smaller agencies, in particular, may find it more economical to use Center facilities for *all* their mechanized information handling than to acquire their own processing equipment.

THE CENTRALIZATION ISSUE

In advocating a Unified Information System with an Information Center as described, the question of centralization requires consideration.

Types of Centralization

It is important to distinguish between two types of centralization: management and information. Neither necessarily demands the existence of the other. The former concerns the way data are *used*; the latter, the way they are *stored*.

Centralized management is a subject completely independent from the Unified Information System. We are not proposing centralization of state and local government organizations or functions in any sense. The Unified Information System does not change existing assignments of management authority and responsibility. The System does not involve, for example, the "monitoring" of city operations by state agencies. Rather, it provides only for the storage and processing of data describing a common environment. The System is specifically designed to accommodate a variety of organizational structures—in themselves either centralized or decentralized—and to furnish them the information they need.

Centralization of information is a recent concept that has developed largely with the application of the electronic computer to data processing problems. As we noted in Chapter 3, state and local governments, although related, form a complex of largely independent organizations. The Unified Information System recognizes this fact and provides only for the central storage and processing of data according to the instructions of participating agencies; it does not in any way prescribe how data are to be used, a matter for each agency to determine for itself. The System simply increases the availability of these data by providing comprehensive information about an environment that is common to many governmental units. The data are stored in a single system because they describe the same persons and parcels, even though agencies use these data for widely differing purposes. The user sends information and receives information on request. Because of rapidly increasing data transmission speeds, such transactions can be essentially instantaneous, thus removing one of the major traditional objections to centralized information storage.

Data To Be Centralized

There are three major bases for storing data in the Center files: commonality of interest in the data; predominance of identity data in a file that also contains specialized data; and preference of an agency to use Center files for storing *all* agency mechanized data.

Commonality of Interest. The first basis is the degree to which interest in the particular items of data is shared by different governmental units and departments. When items of data are of multiple interest, we refer to them as "common data"; when they are of interest only to the agency that collects them, we designate them as "specialized data." Figures 7 and 8 illustrate the contrast between present systems and the Unified Information System in storing common and specialized data.

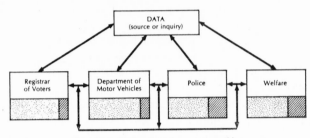

Fig. 7.   Present information files

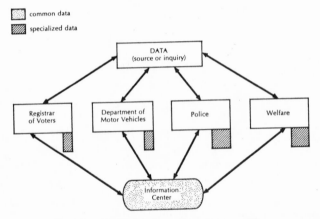

Fig. 8.   Unified Information System files

Under present systems (Fig. 7), data of common interest are stored by the functional agency that collected them. Many of these items of information are not only of common interest but are identical. Figure 8 indicates how such common data would be removed from the individual units (eliminating duplication) and stored at the Unified Information System Center where all agencies would have direct access to them. Thus, any agency desiring common information concerning a person or a parcel of real property need make only one inquiry to the Center, as in Fig. 8, rather than many inquiries to several agencies, as in Fig. 7. Similarly, all agencies would transmit such data to the Center for storage, thus eliminating duplicate filing.

Most of the items of data listed in Chapter 4 on real property and persons are of common interest; some functions, in fact, use only items of common data. As government functions become more interested in information about their environment, the number of items of common data will increase.

We believe that all items on all input documents used by state and local governments should be examined and classified as common or specialized. The classification will not always be clearcut, but it can be guided by the following principles.

First, common interest in any one item of data frequently cannot be determined for that item in isolation. An item of data may be useful to a given function only in combination with several other items. This is particularly true in various kinds of planning activities for which many diverse items are brought together for analysis. For example, the setback of a building may appear to be of specialized interest only to the building regulation department, but, when combined with the assessed value of the land, the uses of surrounding parcels, street width, available off-street parking, and other factors, it may also be useful in making decisions on zoning or street widening.

It is also difficult for someone whose viewpoint is limited to one functional department to determine the value of centralizing information items with which he is concerned. He may think that only he has interest in the data concerned without realizing that other functions might find the data useful if (1) their existence were known and (2) they were accessible.

A second principle in classifying data items as common or specialized is that data describing characteristics of an event and the governmental unit's response to the event tend to be specialized, whereas items describing the environmental objects (person, parcel, or article of property) involved in the event tend to be of common interest. For example, many data are generated and recorded when a fire department responds to a fire alarm. Some describe the characteristics of the event: source of the alarm, area where the fire originated in the building, cause of ignition. Others describe the organizational response to the event: engine company dispatched, extinguishing equipment employed, hoses laid. Finally, some of the data describe the environmental objects involved and the effects on them: address, type of structure, extent of damage, date. These latter items are of common interest and would enter the Unified Information System storage files. This principle is not a clearcut criterion but can be a useful guide in classifying data as common or specialized.

Predominance of Identity Data. The second major basis for determining whether data should be stored centrally in the Unified Information System is the predominance of identity data in a particular file. Many of the records kept by functional departments consist mainly of such identity data about a person, parcel, or article of property. For example, a record in the drivers' license file consists primarily of a person's name, address, age, sex, marital status, and birth date. Included with these identity data are a few items that apply solely to the driver licensing function, such as the driver's license number, license expiration date, and restrictions imposed on the licensee. In terms of numbers of characters and items of information, personal identity data predominate.

Several functions in state and local governments maintain records on persons and parcels wherein identity data are in the majority, and only a minority of items relate exclusively to the function concerned. Voters' registration and vocational licenses are further examples; personal identity data in these files are the same as in the drivers' license file and other analogous files. A similar example involving real property is provided by civil defense records of buildings suitable for shelter facilities. Such records involve a number of items dealing with ownership, location, and structural characteristics, plus only one or two items identifying a particular building to be a shelter facility. The addition of these one or two items of specialized interest to a common central file is highly preferable to compiling a separate and mostly redundant file for civil defense shelters. In short, when identity data and other common items predominate in a particular file, addition of the few specialized items to the unified file and dissolution of the specialized file is an attractive solution.

Agency Preference. A third basis for centralizing the storage of data would be the preference of the individual agency for using the Center facilities for all mechanized data processing and storage. Many agencies might choose to do so rather than to acquire their own equipment.

Specialized Files

Although several major files of data now maintained by various state and local governments would no longer be necessary once the Unified Information System was in operation, some agencies might wish to continue files of certain specialized data within their own jurisdiction. Data on the daily status and treatment of persons in welfare, hospital, and correctional institutions are examples. The data in such files can either be processed for use in agency computers or transmitted to the Center computers for processing according to agency instructions. Common data in the Center files can also be transmitted to local agency computers for processing. This local processing could, for example, involve items of data from both specialized files and the common file. Interaction between the Information Center files and specialized files of individual agencies will be technologically feasible and simple via the communications network subsequently described. We stress that the speed of transmitting and processing data will permit rapid merging of data from two files located hundreds of miles apart. Duplicate filing of common data in specialized files will, therefore, be unnecessary.

CHAPTER SIX

THE UNIFIED INFORMATION SYSTEM:
ACTIVITIES

The major activities of the Unified Information System are the input, output, communication, storage, and processing of data. This chapter discusses these activities and how each would be carried out. The devices and techniques described are illustrative of those which will be available; individual agencies would select those appropriate for their own operations.

INPUT

We shall first consider how data of concern to state and local governments are *generated* and the methods and instruments by which they are *collected*. We will then describe some procedures and devices by which this input process can be improved within the Unified Information System.

Data Generation

Chapter 4 identified scores of information items describing environmental objects. These items derive from events affecting the objects they describe. For example, the data item "zoning" results from an ordinance establishing a zone and applying it to a particular parcel of land. Similarly, data describing a person derive from such events as his birth, marriage, employment, and licensing.

Some events—and their consequent data—occur at the initiative of the citizen; others are initiated by a government agency. For example, if a person wants to vote, he must register on his own initiative, thereby generating a data item about himself (political affiliation) that previously did not exist within the purview of a government agency. This is similarly true of applying for a driver's license, constructing a building, or buying a car. Governments also undertake actions which generate data about persons and property, such as the field surveys of the assessor, public health, agriculture, and fire departments, and the many actions affecting public rights of way and other physical public facilities.

Whether an event is initiated by a citizen or by a government agency, the information generated by or associated with its occurrence frequently is of multiple interest to state and local governments. Thus, when there is a birth, a fire, or an auto registration, agencies besides the one originally recording the data are concerned. Frequently, different aspects of the same event are of concern to different agencies. A structural fire is, of course, the immediate concern of the fire department, but the assessor needs to know what the fire loss was so that he can accordingly adjust the assessed value of the improvements affected. Likewise, police, traffic, and public works functions may all be interested in a particular traffic accident. In some cases, interested functions are within the same parent jurisdiction, such as departments in a city government. In others, functions in several jurisdictions are concerned, such as common interest at all government levels in land use and persons' addresses.

Data Collection Methods and Instruments

Data generated by an event must be collected. In state and local governments, the collection process uses four major input methods. Associated with each method are instruments—generally pieces of paper on which the data are originally recorded. These methods, and typical events and instruments associated with each, are as follows:

1. *Observation of an event or object by government personnel.* This may be a visual observation and recording of the event and/or the asking of questions and recording of answers.

Typical Events	*Instruments*
Traffic accident	Investigation report
Fire	Investigation report
Property appraisal	Inspection report
Crime	Inspection report
Sanitation inspection	Inspection report
Personal confinement or release from confinement (for correctional, probational, health, or welfare purposes)	Status report, admission, release

2. *Report of an event by a citizen or by someone on behalf of a citizen.* Such reports are generally submitted on government-prescribed forms, often by mail.

Typical Events	Instruments
Birth, death, marriage	Certificate
Receipt of taxable income or sale	Tax report
Industrial accident	Accident report
Agricultural crop production	Crop report
Sale of property	Deed
Occurrence of certain communicable diseases	Morbidity report

3. *Application or registration by a citizen in connection with government service or regulation.* Generally, the citizen visits a government office and gives information on prescribed forms. Application and registration by mail are also common.

Typical Events	Instruments
School enrollment	Registration form
Registration to vote	Voter registration form
Construction of building	Building permit
Request for license	Application form
Request for welfare or unemployment assistance	Request form and follow-up investigation report

4. *Administrative actions by government agencies.*

Typical Events	Instruments
Zoning	Ordinance
Annexation, incorporation	Ordinance
Street widening or resurfacing	Report and plans
Court decision	Decree, warrant
Public facilities acquisition and construction	Maps, administrative documents
Assessment for improvements	Assessment roll and bonds
Assignment of house number (street address)	Internal administrative document

Some events create data which are collected by a combination of methods, especially when a citizen initiates an event that is subsequently investigated by a government agency.

In state and local governments, each of these methods typically conveys data to only one department or unit. The specific items collected about each event are generally selected to serve only the functional purpose of the agency responsible for collecting them. A basic principle of the Unified Information System is that all four methods and the instruments associated with them will be considered and designed to supply input to a comprehensive information system serving many functions, departments, and agencies. This means that each phase of the input process must be viewed from a much broader perspective than has traditionally been possible.

It also means that careful attention must be given to ensuring accuracy in each phase of the input process.

The Unified Information System is designed to fulfill four major objectives with respect to input:

1. To reduce duplicate collection of the same items of information.

2. To increase the number of government functions and units whose information needs are supplied by data items collected in connection with each event.

3. To reduce errors in data recording.

4. To reduce the need for manual transcription of data by facilitating their original collection in a form suitable for all future uses, or in a manner which enables them to be processed for use automatically rather than manually.

In describing implementation of these objectives, we shall discuss data collection criteria, data collection media, data editing, and operations of the input system.

Data Collection Criteria

Government officers can usually specify the data they need or would like to have to perform their functions. The problem then becomes one of collection.

The first input objective specifies that we want to reduce duplicate collection of information items by governmental units. Once the Unified Information System is in operation, interrogation of the System files will replace a great deal of original collection. Most events generate little "new" information—data not to be found in any state or local government file. For example, most data items on a report of a particular welfare application, traffic accident, building inspection, or license application already exist in some file. New events generally involve objects about which considerable descriptive data already exist. Ideally, data already on file should not be collected again; only new data created by the new event should be gathered. Under existing systems, however, duplicate data are collected for several reasons:

1. Existence of the data elsewhere is not known to the function having a present need for the data.

2. The data filed elsewhere are inaccessible or in a form that is unsuitable for use by the function presently needing them.

3. It is mechanically easier to collect the data again than to retrieve them from the file in which they are presently located.

4. The data must be gathered in order to identify correctly the objects (person or property) involved in a particular event.

The storage and output capabilities of the Unified Information System described below will make reasons 1, 2, and 3 considerably less valid. Items resulting from reason 4 can be fewer because of the validity checks made possible by the computer. It will often be easier to interrogate the System files for existing data than to record extensive data about the objects involved in connection with each event.

What does this mean in practical operations? Simply that in collecting information about such events as welfare applications, real property appraisal investigations, and institution reception processing, the first step in "information gathering" will be file interrogation rather than original data observation and recording. The inquiry devices described below will enable basic identity information, such as name, Social Security number, address, date of birth, and sex, to be entered in the device, and from it a print-out or display of all relevant data on file about that person or parcel can be rapidly produced for review. This information can then be verified and supplemented by observation or interrogation without the need for duplicate collection of data items already on file.

Although this precollection retrieval process will reduce much duplication, some will continue either because it is mechanically easier (as in the case of data collected at random in the field by such means as traffic citations and voters' registration) or because it is necessary to identify correctly the objects affected. Any such duplicate data will be automatically compared with data on file prior to storage, and then discarded if redundant.

The second input system objective is to increase the number of state and local government functions whose information needs are supplied by data items collected in connection with each event. Earlier, we described the role of the Information Center in articulating these needs. Let us discuss how the four major methods by which data flow into state and local governments serve this objective. It is immediately clear that not all methods discussed earlier are equally suitable. Method 1—observation of an event or object by government personnel—is the method through which the greatest number and variety of information items can be gathered. Method 3 is the next best in terms of maximizing the number of items collected in connection with a specific event, and method 2 is the poorest. Method 4 is of a different character but permits wide latitude in the selection of items to be gathered.

In practical terms, it is not reasonable to expect a citizen to fill out a five-page questionnaire every time a license is requested, a parcel of land sold, an address changed, or a death reported. On the other hand, when a government officer is "on the scene" and can record the data items himself, many more can be collected. This means that the information-collecting responsibilities of the numerous field personnel employed by government agencies must be considerably broadened. Thus, for example, fire, health, agriculture, licensing, welfare, law enforcement, voters' registration, natural resources, and assessor personnel, in gathering data about events and conditions of primary concern to their respective departments, should also be responsible for gathering data about these events and conditions for the use of other functions and units.

Often, most of the items collected by the various methods to describe objects and events are the same. In these cases, parallel observation or application-registration can be avoided by enlarging the uses to which a single observation or application-registration is put. For example, there is no logical reason why reporting a change of address for the primary concern of the motor vehicle department and simple reregistering to vote (both of which are concerned with the address of a specific person) cannot be accomplished by one piece of paper conveying information sworn to by the citizen. In the Unified Information System, this information could enter a common file to which both functions would have access. Duplicate collection and storage is eliminated and the citizen's task made easier. Various validity checks by a computer program could reduce to negligible proportions the chance of error or fraud in reporting and recording the information.

In considering data collection criteria, one must constantly focus on the information items themselves and ask how each can best be collected. Each item listed in Chapter 4 should be examined and the possible sources of each identified. Wherever information passes into a government office for any purpose, the method and instrument involved should be examined as a possible input source for other data. Utility payment stubs, tax returns, license and permit applications—every contact between the citizen and any state or local government agency is a potential source for data input. Especially where regular reports, applications, or observations are made, the documents involved should be considered as inputs to the entire state and local government information system, not merely to the department and unit with an immediate interest. For each such method, the entire range of information items available (defined in the broadest terms) should be considered and a determination made of what data input is feasible (defined again in terms of the most comprehensive use to which the items will be put). This does not mean, of course, the random collection of data for their own sake but rather that data collection should be viewed in light of the needs of the total range of state and local governments.

The number of separate field inspections by different government employees and the number of separate reports, applications, and registrations required of the citizen could be substantially reduced by such integration of data item collection. And given the storage and access capabilities of the Unified Information System, the various departments would have more information available to them more rapidly than present systems permit.

Data Collection Media

Here we are concerned with the physical process of accurately recording data. For the foreseeable future, paper documents will remain the major original input instrument for collecting environmental data used by state and local governments. This fact is emphasized, since in many business and industrial systems, automatic input as a byproduct of another operation is often possible. For example, in manufacturing processes, the equipment involved can often automatically generate data describing the goods produced. For data describing the state and local governmental *environment*, however, original input will probably continue to be by paper documents.

It should be added that many source documents themselves have intrinsic legal value beyond that of the data they contain. For example, the certifications signed by applicants for such services as welfare assistance and building permits must be preserved. We shall discuss the filing of such documents in the subsequent section on storage; here we are concerned only with the data recorded on the documents.

Given our input system objectives and the probable permanency of paper original source documents, we turn to how the specific items of data are recorded on the documents concerned. The first three input methods usually involve data originally recorded by hand:

(1) Observation of an event or object by government personnel
(2) Report of an event by a citizen affecting him or his property
(3) Application or registration by a citizen in connection with service or regulation.

A review of the instruments conveying information about events in these three categories suggests that recording by hand will probably continue to be the predominant form of original data collection. It will be many years before machines can correctly and economically read the ordinary handwriting of millions of people. Information recorded in handwriting, therefore, will probably not be acceptable for direct input into the System in the 1970-75 period. However, this is not a serious problem because most of the data items to be handled by the System need not be originally recorded in handwriting. The few that do can be manually transcribed into an acceptable input format or hand*printed*. Let us consider the variety of input media that will be available.

Punch cards will probably continue to be a major input medium. They can be key punched from original source-documents, or can themselves be the source-documents. In this latter case, information can be entered by marking prespecified spaces or by punching out prespecified holes. This is particularly useful in providing a reporting medium for such field personnel as police officers, license and agriculture inspectors, and probation officers. The cards are then read automatically. In the Unified Information System, punch cards could be prepared by the participating agencies and mailed to the Information Center for reading. Large agencies might have their own card readers, which would transmit data from cards to the Center via the communications network (described on p. 73).

Punch paper tape would provide a medium for data generated or summarized by the operations of another machine. It is also useful for assembling data from many punch cards.

Optical reading input is promising. Optical readers will be able to read information recorded in typewritten, printed, and carefully hand*printed* characters. No special writing instrument or ink will be required for reliable performance in the 1970-75 period. In the Unified Information System, optical readers could be located in larger agencies with high input volumes. Smaller agencies could use the readers of neighboring larger agencies, share such a reader jointly, or transmit facsimile images or microfilms of source documents to the Center for optical reading there. Departments with many field offices could also use the facsimile or microfilm methods to transmit document images from field offices to central headquarters for optical reading and subsequent transmission of data to the Center. The System is fully flexible to fit the operational and economic requirements of each participating agency.

All input media will require improvements in the design and use of forms on which the data are recorded. Some of the specific considerations in the design of forms which will provide input to an automatic information system are as follows:

1. *Phrasing of information requested*—"blanks to be filled in," such as name, birth date, address—so that the specific data to be supplied are (a) clearly understandable and unambiguous; and (b) amenable as much as possible to yes/no, multiple choice, or numerical answers. Except for data which only words can supply—name, for example—possible alternative answers should be prespecified so that the information can be provided by a mark in an appropriate space. Many more data items than might be supposed can be supplied in this form or by numbers, particularly the kinds of data items that would enter the Unified Information System. Extensive codification and careful wording of information requested would enable almost all the data items listed in Chapter 4 to be supplied in a prespecified or numerical form. Narrative, "case history" statements may be part of the source documents, but the key data—especially those intended for storage in the System—should be supplied in categorical or numerical form. In Chapter 5 we discussed the need for

standardization and coding of data items. Here we simply emphasize that original input documents should strive for a data collection format employing these characteristics.

2. *Standardization in the placement of data items.* In order to "sense" correctly or read a particular item, such as "offense charged," "year born," or "soil type," optical devices must find the item consistently in the same place on the same type of form. This standardization of item position does not need to extend to all forms used by all agencies in the System. It is sufficient that all like documents of one agency used to report a specific type of event be standardized. The input devices used by that agency or the Center would be set to accept that agency's documents. This setting could be changed for different forms, such as traffic citations, building permits, and birth certificates. Where narrative statements such as ordinances, court decrees, administrative regulations, and case histories were present, it would be necessary to extract from the narrative those items of data to be entered in the System. This would be a prerequisite to efficient optical reading of these data. Extraction could be done automatically by setting aside a portion of the document wherein such data would be placed.

Data Editing

Editing helps to ensure the completeness and correctness of data prior to their storage or processing. Both humans and machines are needed in the editing process, although automatic devices are becoming increasingly important.

A major requirement in the Unified Information System is the assignment of correct parcel and Social Security numbers to any data describing real property or persons. Thus, it is essential that data describing fires, accidents, buildings, crops, taxes, zones, etc., be associated with the correct property parcels, and that licenses, addresses, political affiliations, warrants, employment earnings, etc., be associated with the correct persons.

With respect to real property, it is unlikely that the parcel number can be recorded as part of the data originally collected on most source-documents. It is an internal number seldom known either to the public or to many of the data collection agencies. Rather, it must be assigned from street address or legal description items listed on the documents describing the event affecting the parcel. Most input documents affecting real property identify parcels by street address. Computer programs can automatically convert street addresses to parcel numbers, and perform self-checking operations to ensure accuracy in cross indexing. Documents containing data which affect the title or change the dimensions of a parcel of real property (deeds, tracts, assessments, lot splits, etc.) will often require manual review, since involved legal descriptions are frequently used to identify the property concerned. Such review would take place at the point where parcel numbers are assigned. Where parcels are divided or combined, review of all data items in the record(s) of the parcel(s) affected would be necessary to create the successor parcel record(s). This review could be performed by Information Center personnel or by employees in a local participating agency. After the proper number is created or assigned, the automatic input process would proceed. As in the case of addresses, where the parcel is a numbered lot in a numbered tract, automatic optical sensing and cross indexing to parcel number will be possible.

Because of its uniformity and comprehensiveness, the Social Security number is the best numerical identifier of people. It should be included as an information item on all input documents containing data describing a person. If he has no Social Security number (this condition will become less frequent as the coverage and use of Social Security numbers expand), a number code can be constructed based on certain of his identifying characteristics, such as the spelling of his name, sex, date of birth, race, and eye color. Such codes have already been developed and could be used to supplement the Social Security number as an additional validity check to ensure that data are correctly connected to the right person.

Besides ensuring the proper connection of data to the objects they describe, the editing process must review the data themselves for completeness and correctness. The review for completeness is a mechanical check that "all the appropriate blanks" on a form are filled in, that is, all the data called for in a transaction are supplied or their unavailability explicitly noted. This is a simple, automatic process for a computer program.

Correctness is more difficult to ensure. Some checks for correctness would be made at the Center where the data are stored; this is discussed below in the section on processing. At any point in the editing process, documents rejected by the equipment because of incorrect or incomplete data will be routed for persons to review and edit. Manual review of documents will sometimes be necessary prior to entry of the data they contain into the System. Particularly when data are extracted from complex narratives, a data review specialist should review documents to ensure the correctness of data to be entered in the System. Large agencies may find it desirable to establish a special personnel class for this function; smaller agencies can reasonably assign it to regular clerical personnel.

To ensure accuracy in editing before data are transmitted for storage or processing, devices which display the data for visual review can be used. These devices read the document and display the data on a screen as read. A human operator can then quickly scan the image for obvious errors before pushing a "transmit" button.

Together, the various input editing checks described here and in the section below on processing can give the information stored in the Unified Information System considerably greater accuracy than present manual systems permit.

Input System Operations

The Unified Information System will have input locations that are organizationally independent, geographically remote, and functionally unrelated.

In summary, we envision that every governmental unit participating in the System will have stations to enter data into the System. These stations will consist of keyboard, punch card, paper tape, and/or optical reading devices in combination with data transmission terminal equipment. Stations in the participating agencies will also permit inquiries to be made via keyboard devices and will provide both printed and display output. Such stations will, of course, have flexible and different capabilities, depending on the requirements of the agency.

Data from many source-documents will be read automatically by devices at these stations. Key punching of nonmachine-readable documents can enter the remaining data into the System. To these stations would come, therefore, police reports, birth certificates, building permits, deeds, license applications, face sheets on social welfare cases, crop production reports, traffic citations, warrants, assessment reports, and other documents. Specified data would be extracted from these for transmittal to the Information Center.

Stations located in different organizational units would have different capabilities. Some would only be able to accept data for input and transmission; others might also be able to do some raw-data editing. Large governmental units, such as urban counties, would undoubtedly have many input stations—even several in a single department. Such stations would be connected by communication links with the Information Center, either directly or via departmental or jurisdictional facilities that could batch, edit, summarize, or aggregate the data prior to transmittal.

The input stations could also handle data of specialized or internal concern to the agency involved. For example, business license applications containing both environmental and internal data could be automatically edited to segregate these two types of data. Internal data used to issue the license—such as the fee charged—would be processed for the local department and the license issued. One pass through the input station would enable the data on the application to be reviewed for completeness and correctness, preparation and recording of the license, posting of local agency revenue records, and transmission of common data describing the person and/or parcel involved to Information Center files. As discussed further in the section on processing, the computing involved in these operations could be performed either by local or Center equipment.

Output

Closely associated with the input of data is output—reporting of the results of processing or the status of any items filed in storage. Output presents data for use. The stations that accept input could, and often would, also be equipped to provide output, which would usually take the form of either printed copy or visual display. Printed output could be supplied in such forms as tax bills, address labels, precinct lists, licenses, and complete or selected listings of data on file about individual or aggregate persons or parcels. Inquiries for specific items of data—the age of a building, the date of last sanitation inspection, the years of school completed—would often be satisfied by a visual display of the requested information without printed copy. Stations for accepting such inquiries and reporting the requested data would likely be located in executive offices as well as in working areas of various departments.

Requests for data, either from storage or from processing, require exact identification of persons and parcels and specification of the data desired or the process to be executed on the specified data. The following example illustrates how the station could supply requested output. Several activities of local governments require that property owners be notified that specified actions are contemplated, such as annexation, weed cleaning, and zoning. In the case of zoning, owners of property within a specified distance of the property affected must generally be notified of the action proposed and the date of the public hearing. If mailed notice is used (and it is used increasingly), present manual systems involve laborious identification of the proper parcels and owners and the printing and addressing of notices. In the Unified Information System, a technician could simply draw a line with a compass encircling all parcels within, say, 300 feet of the property affected by the proposed action. Parcel number(s) representing this property would be entered in the station with a coded program instruction similar to the following: "Find legal owners for each of these parcels, print out notices specifying a proposed change of zone for parcel 27 389 476—also known as 123 Main Street—from C1 to C2; state that public hearing on this proposed action will be (time, date, place); print address labels." Eventually, even the parcels to be notified could be determined automatically by the computer from parcel size calculations.

Mechanically, requests for output would be submitted to the station in the same form as basic inputs, usually key stroke or printed messages coded for optical sensing. Stations could be equipped to handle all or only certain kinds of output and inquiry. The question of restricted access to preserve the confidentiality of certain data was considered earlier. Here we emphasize the capability of the stations to report in any specified form any data that are on file or are the result of any processing. Each agency would thus receive data in the format it had specified.

COMMUNICATIONS

Without rapid, economical communications, the Unified Information System would be impossible. Chapter 2 described the probable advances in communication technology over the next decade; here we discuss how they can be used in the Unified Information System.

Communication supplies the channels through which the data flow among other elements of the system: input, storage, processing, and output. The Unified Information System is characterized by centralized storage and processing and decentralized input and output. Centralized storage and processing would be performed at the Information Center; input and output in the participating agencies. The Center and the agencies would be linked by communication lines. As illustrated in Fig. 6 (on p. 50), these lines would connect the Center both to the governmental units—state, county, city, township, or district—and to their constituent departments. Data could, therefore, flow directly between the source department and the Center or via the governmental unit involved. The major considerations in these connection arrangements would be the interest of the parent unit in reviewing or batching data gathered by a department prior to their transmission to the Center, and the interest of economies in having fewer input stations in a single jurisdiction. In the Unified Information System, such decisions would be made by each participating agency. A state-wide system would accommodate local variations in such arrangements. Let us, therefore, turn to the characteristics of the communications network.

Communications Network

We believe that regular telephone network facilities will be suitable for communicating most of the data in the Unified Information System. Except for the largest agencies with very high volumes of data transmission, no separate, private-line circuits will be necessary. The common-carrier message network which carries voice will also carry digital data fast and accurately enough to meet the requirements of state and local governments.

This prospect significantly simplifies the Unified Information System.

Every agency and department has telephone facilities which, together with input/output station devices, will enable data transmission anywhere in the System. Where very high volumes of data are transmitted between the Center and a large jurisdiction—say, a city of 500,000 population—a private channel for data communications may be more economical. We believe, however, that for most units of government, their departments, and field offices, the regular telephone network will be entirely adequate. Teletype service can also be used.

Whether data are transmitted by wire or by microwave is of no concern to the sender or receiver. As in ordinary voice transmission, common carriers will use a mix of modes at different times, depending on traffic volume, maintenance schedules, and other factors incidental to the user. The sender will dial the receiver, obtain "ready" clearance, and push a transmit button to communicate the data. Such an operation will often be automatic.

Message Characteristics

Items of data are conveyed in the form of messages, which also contain such control information as (1) originating station or Center; (2) precedence indicator (priority inquiry/response, routine, or file maintenance transaction); (3) date/time indicator; and (4) beginning and end of message symbols.

Messages will originate either at the Center or at a station in one of hundreds of locations. Devices at any of these points will ensure the presence of all the required message components before transmission. The content of a message from a station could include items of information and also instructions as to whether the Center should file the items or process them in some specified way. Alternately, a message could contain either a request for information stored in the Center or instructions for processing data already in the Center files.

Message Handling

Thousands of messages will flow daily among various elements of the Unified Information System, carrying different priorities: rapid response inquiries and responses, routine requests and resulting output, and file maintenance transactions. The network must and will have the capability to transmit these according to their priority. At each station and at the Center, devices will (a) temporarily store data waiting for transmission and (b) initiate "priority interrupt" actions to enable high-priority messages to be transmitted without delay. For example, a station in the city of Pasadena may be transmitting to the Center certain data from the day's accumulation of building permits. Midway through this process a citizen wishes to know the record owner of a property parcel in the city. The request is entered into the station and the building permit data transmission is halted (for a fraction of a second) while this priority request is transmitted. When the requested data are located in the Center storage files, the station is notified, and the building permit operation is halted again while the data are transmitted. This entire process is handled automatically by the switching hardware of the communications system. Such a priority-interrupt process will enable "real time" data communication between the Center and the agencies in those cases in which rapid response is required. The regular telephone network will also permit parallel communication between the Center and any government agency via several circuits.

We believe such concerns as "serial" versus "random" access and "batch" versus "in-line" processing will become less critical as equipment capabilities increase. In particular, input data seldom will need to be sorted by type or batched at the station prior to transmittal. Such data may be transmitted in the order and at the time which best suits the convenience of the agency where the station is located. At the Center, data will be ordered for optimum filing and processing. Certain economies in transmission may result from longer messages; so routine and file maintenance messages may be accumulated for transmission during night hours, leaving the circuits free for priority inquiries and responses during the day. In addition to telephonic data transmission, the regular mails can often be used for communicating volumes of lower priority data between the Center and participating agencies.

STORAGE

A basic premise of the Unified Information System is that many environmental data items should be stored centrally. Centralized storage is a natural outgrowth of the multiple use of environmental data by state and local governments. Simply explained, centralized storage means that data from several different agencies (both governmental units and their constituent departments) are filed in a common depository. In the Unified Information System, the Information Center is the depository.

In this section we shall discuss the files in which data items should be stored; the accessibility of data stored in them; and the storing of *documents* as contrasted to *data*.

Data Files

The Unified Information System involves two basic files of data describing the state and local governmental environment. These files and the records in them contain information items relating to real property and persons. The basic unit for real property is the individual parcel (with a separate real property file for street sections); for people, the basic unit is the individual person.

Use of the parcel and the person as the basic units departs from many data systems which store data originally in some aggregate form, such as census tract, administrative district, or socioeconomic group. We believe the person and the parcel are preferable units because data *originate* according to these units. Fires, building permits, births, licenses, and all other events involve individual parcels or individual persons when they occur, and the relevant data are generated and collected. If the system stores data by these basic units, they may then be aggregated in any grouping. Aggregate storage, on the other hand, may preclude some kinds of groupings. For example, if original data about real property are stored only by census tract aggregates, they cannot be grouped by voting precincts within that tract. Storage of data by parcel and person, however, permits maximum flexibility in aggregation. Furthermore, some government operations, such as taxation and licensing, must deal with data by these basic units.

The Unified Information System, then, keeps a record for each parcel of real property and street section, and a record for each person with whom any government agency has had some contact. The number of different items of information included in each record would vary. Some items would be present for all parcels and persons, others only if the event they describe has happened to the person or parcel involved. Thus, although there is an owner for every parcel, data on tax delinquencies are recorded only when they occur. In addition to substantive data, each record would contain control information to indicate the agency from which the data are received and "as of" dates when they are not clear from other data items in the record. This information applies only to a portion of the items, but to that portion it is usually essential.

In some cases, several items of data would be included to describe completely a particular event or condition; in others, a single item would reveal the existence of additional data in another specified file. For example, the "extractive data" item in a real property record could indicate that oil was extracted from the parcel and refer to the file in which further data are located. The additional data could be stored in manual, punch card, or electronic files by various agencies and could be obtained via the communications network. In such cases, the parcel file would serve essentially as a complete index system to all data about the parcel in state and local government files.

There would, therefore, be a wide divergence in the number of items for each record in a state-wide storage system. It would probably range from 50 to 70 items per parcel for real property—the higher numbers for urban areas; from 25 to 35 for street sections; and from 20 to 40 for persons. The number of characters required for storing each item would depend largely on the extent of coding, but would average about 9 per item for persons, 5 for parcels, and 17 for street sections. In the following chapter on System costs, we have estimated the size of state-wide files of persons and real property in five states. These calculations are based on an average of 30 items per record for persons and 60 items per record for parcels. It is assumed that there will be a record for every parcel and for 90 per cent of the persons. For two states—one large and one small—the following figures indicate the estimated number of characters in System storage files for persons and parcels:

	California	New Hampshire
Person file	3,819,150,000	147,420,000
Parcel file	1,650,300,000	80,100,000
Total characters	5,469,450,000	227,520,000

Although free interaction among them would be simple, person, parcel, and street section files would be organized separately in the Information Center. The size of each file, rather than the three together, is, therefore, significant for storage purposes. A system capable of storing several times the number of characters shown above, with acceptable access to the data, will be technologically and economically feasible in the 1970-75 period.

Accessibility

Accessibility to the stored data is a major consideration in any centralized data storage system. Time and format are the major dimensions of accessibility. In our earlier description of the input/output station, we noted the variety of formats in which stored data could be supplied to users. Although data describing persons and parcels could be stored electronically by the Center in the general order listed in Chapter 4, they would be supplied at these remote stations in any order and in any output format specified by the user.

Since time is the more significant dimension of accessibility in the Unified Information System, let us consider the time requirements for data used by state and local governments. A basic requirement of the Unified Information System is that it supply information to a user at least as fast as he can get it from separate individual systems. This requirement must be viewed in a perspective that includes total costs and actual needs. For example, some manual systems can keep certain data rapidly accessible at a very high cost of input or processing. Property ownership records are an example. Often a person can learn the owner of a parcel from assessment books in five minutes (often, however, he cannot!), but the total cost of hand processing and posting these data is very high. A doubling of the access time to ten minutes would not be unreasonable if balanced against the savings in input time, accuracy—especially in the currency of data—and cost, which a more automatic system would afford. When specifying the time urgency of data, the tendency to exaggerate the importance of rapid response must be avoided. The costs of the delay are often not very great, especially when measured against savings on input and processing.

Access time should depend on the use to which the data are put. Few state and local government functions need rapid access to environmental data. For purposes of analysis let us limit the term "rapid access" to cases in which no more than three minutes can elapse between an inquiry by a remote input station and the Center's response. *Average* access time would be substantially less, although three minutes is realistic in terms of state and local government requirements. Let us refer to requests for data requiring such rapid access as *priority inquiries*; these would generally involve retrieval of data items in the form in which they were stored. Processing would seldom be involved. In state and local government functions, simple priority inquiries would be made mainly for basic identity information items, such as the ownership of a parcel or the address of a person. Need for the entire record of a person or parcel would be uncommon but, if it were required, it could be retrieved and reported within priority time constraints.

Besides these priority inquiries, most governmental units require the output of stored and processed data on a less urgent basis. Many government functions use environmental data in periodic activities that either recur regularly or can be planned well in advance. Tax billing, periodic license renewal, issuance of public hearing notices, land-use inventory, precinct list preparation—none of these applications requires rapid access to the data. With careful planning, several days or even weeks may pass between the request and the time the data are needed in a specified output format. Such less urgent requests may be defined as requiring *routine access*. In many cases, routine data requests require data processing in contrast to simple retrieval. As the examples above indicate, they also frequently involve many persons or parcels, whereas priority requests usually involve one or a few.

In a state-wide system, thousands of requests would come to the Center daily from hundreds of input stations. The storage files would need to be organized in order to respond to priority requests in the allotted time while meeting the specified deadlines of less urgent, routine requests. Today's electronic systems employ "priority interrupt" features to accomplish this on a limited scale. We believe that the large-capacity parallel-access storage devices in the next decade will permit priority inquiries and routine requests as well as processing actions to be handled on files of the magnitude we have specified in what amounts to simultaneous operation. This will be possible because the basic file can be organized so that all items will *always* be available for interrogation. When certain items are needed for processing, they will be "read out" into the *working* storage of the computer which will do the processing, while still being retained in the central *file* storage of the system. For example, if certain data are needed to be printed out as precinct lists for Madera County, these data will be extracted from the file storage and transmitted to the processing facility—in either the local agency or Information Center—where the lists will be prepared in accordance with the requirements of Madera County. These same data, which are in effect reproduced elsewhere for processing, will also remain in the Center file storage. The same items of data will, therefore, be available for many different processing uses, while remaining continuously available in the Center files for interrogation.

In addition to thousands of daily requests for priority and routine access to items in the Center files, there will be many transactions reflecting changes in already stored items and reporting additional items. These "file maintenance" transactions will automatically update Center files. This updating can occur on a daily basis during night hours when interrogation demands are at a minimum. The need for temporarily holding these file maintenance transactions as well as file access requests will be satisfied by buffering devices, such as magnetic drums or tapes. These devices will receive both updating data and access requests, order them, and direct them to the proper part of the file at the proper time in accordance with specified priorities. First, urgent inquiries will be given highest priority, next, routine requests and those involving processing, and then, finally, file maintenance transactions.

Historical Files

The person and real property files of the Unified Information System would contain primarily the most recent information items as well as data describing past events of current interest. However, when a particular item —perhaps an address, land use, or the taxes paid in a prior year—is superseded by new information, the older information can be placed in separate "historical files." Such files would have slower access than the current files but would be maintained within the System to aid research and analysis as well as to permit reconstruction of the current files if they were damaged or destroyed.

Document Storage

The Unified Information System is primarily concerned with storing data expressed in digital form: numbers, letters, and symbols. Almost all of these data are originally recorded on pieces of paper, as we noted in discussing input. In many cases, these pieces of paper (documents) themselves have value beyond that of the data they contain, often because of signatures validating the actions reported in the documents. Both documents and data must, therefore, be stored. Requirements for the storage of documents are generally based on either legal or administrative considerations. In the legal category are such documents as birth, marriage, and death certificates, deeds, and ordinances. Most of these (or photographic copies of them) are preserved indefinitely. For administrative control and audit, government agencies also preserve many of the documents on which environmental data are originally recorded: building permits, social agency interview face sheets, traffic citations, inspection reports, license applications. Some of these documents are destroyed after a period of years; some are kept indefinitely.

The input system described earlier is designed to collect only data, not documents. We believe that the various government agencies can and should retain custody of the documents from which data are entered into the Unified Information System. By doing so, they can always verify and audit the correctness of information pertaining to their jurisdiction in the System. The storage of such documents can, of course, be vastly improved by such techniques as microfilming or video tape recording, but the principle of retaining them apart from the Unified Information System should be observed. This principle would continue the current practice of each agency's keeping its own document files. The Unified Information System can serve as a master index to the location of documents by noting on person and parcel records which documents are in the possession of which agencies. Agencies requiring a document can query the System for its existence and location, and obtain it (via facsimile transmission or mail) from the appropriate agency.

To be sure, these documents would have little use, since, except in a few cases (such as court records), data—not documents—are used. Most data would be much more accessible and usable in digital form either from the files of the Unified Information System or from the specialized files of the agency concerned. In a sense, documents generally become archives when their relevant data have been stored in accessible electronic files. These files, both common and specialized, will contain the data items actually *used* in the functions of state and local governments.

PROCESSING

In the Unified Information System, data will be processed for two general purposes: (1) to ensure their validity prior to storage in the System files and (2) to prepare them for a use specified by one of the participating agencies.

Validity Processing

Validity processing is designed to verify the correctness and completeness of reported data by various consistency checks. Often called editing, these checks compare data items in order to detect errors in reporting. For example, reported addresses can be automatically checked to ensure that the digits in a house number fall within the numbers in existence for the street on which the address is reported; or a message reporting the destruction of a building by fire can be validated internally by checking to see that the stored record for the parcel concerned confirms the presence of a building on that parcel. If the record shows no building, the computer reports the discrepancy for investigation. Perhaps a wrong parcel number has been given; perhaps the data describing the construction of the building were never stored. In any case, validity checks can automatically alert the agency to the problem, and thereby initiate an inquiry.

Besides checking for consistency, validity processing can review data for reasonableness. For example, the reported ages of persons can be checked for plausibility according to the events in which they are supposedly involved. Thus, data reporting the enrollment of a 45-year-old in elementary school, or an 11-year-old's application for unemployment insurance, could be automatically rejected as "unreasonable." Many imaginative checks can be employed to verify the internal validity of reported data. Several large systems, including Social Security and airlines reservation operations, regularly apply various automatic input correction routines. Validity processing would, in the Unified Information System, be performed primarily at the Center.

User Processing

The vast bulk of data processing is devoted to preparing data for use by a government agency. As noted earlier, data are used both in the form in which they are stored—for example, the address of a person—and in a form resulting from their manipulation in relation to other items. This manipulation process involves comparisons, computations, aggregations, summations, correlations, and other actions that permit data to be used in clerical and managerial operations. The product is often printed copy: tax bills, licenses, election notices, checks, or simply reports for administrative evaluation. Increasingly, we believe, it will be data displayed on a screen for one-time visual review.

In all of these cases, data are manipulated according to explicit decision rules. A basic premise of the Unified Information System is that these rules are written to execute the instructions of the agency which uses the resulting information. The computer, whether in the Center or in an agency, simply follows these instructions, which do not need to be standardized in any sense between agencies. For example, property tax bills are, and will continue to be, issued by assessors in many different counties, cities, and districts. Different procedures, or rules, are followed in different agencies even though the data may be similar. In processing, the Unified Information System will always follow the rules specified by the user. No centralized rule formulation of any sort is contemplated for the Unified Information System.

The speed of computers in executing explicit decision rules is already great, and will grow to exceed any foreseeable demands in performing information processing for state and local governments. We anticipate that much of the processing for these governments will be done by high capacity computers in the Information Center, where large volume and complex programs can be executed more efficiently. State-wide licensing for drivers and vocations, tax processing for income and property, unemployment and welfare payment programs, and other such data processing functions can be more suitably performed centrally, although the printed output would be provided via mail or communications networks at any remote station in the using department. Large-scale land-use inventories and research analyses of many data also would be processed best at the Center. Computers will, of course, be able to process several applications simultaneously, and so no delay is inherent in this centralized processing.

We expect, however, that processing capability will continue to be required in many governmental jurisdictions. Specialized environmental data as well as internal data will often be processed locally, and occasionally common data may be transmitted from the Center for local processing in combination with specialized data stored locally. Similarly, the Center can process specialized data at an agency's request. In either case, data transmission speeds will permit rapid communication of data between remote files. Bringing environmental and internal data together would be required, for example, in analysis of police manpower activity in relation to neighborhood characteristics on various beats. We therefore foresee that the Unified Information System will embrace both centralized and decentralized processing capability. The bulk of large volume and complex processing will be performed centrally; that of specialized and internal processing will be done in the various units of state and local government. Some agencies, of course, will elect to have the Information Center do *all* their mechanized data handling.

Graphic Data

The Unified Information System is primarily concerned with digital data (letters, numbers, and symbols), the type used principally in state and local government functions. Some data, on the other hand, are represented graphically. Graphic data are most familiar in maps used to describe real property and the structures upon or within it. Photographs, pictures, graphs, and charts are also forms of graphic data.

Within state and local governments, many graphic data are gathered, stored, and used in common, especially in civil engineering maps. Duplication usually results from unawareness of the existence of prior data (maps) or from unsatisfactory means of retrieval. The Unified Information System provides improvements in both of these areas.

First, in each real property parcel or street section record, there can be a notation of the significant maps of all agencies which affect or include that parcel or street section. An inquiry will produce a list of agencies that have mapped the area; this list will include the parcel(s) or street section(s), and data on when and why the mapping was done. In this respect, the Center real property file will serve as a comprehensive map index.

Second, graphic data can eventually be stored in the Center files and reproduced at remote locations via the communication network. Facsimile transmission of engineering maps will be feasible in the 1970's. These maps could be stored centrally on microfilm or video tape, transmitted over the network, and reproduced at remote locations, an arrangement that would enable both a reduction in the bulk of local storage and a consolidation of maps showing different characteristics of the same parcel or street section. Transmission of facsimile images from one agency to another will also be feasible.

The Unified Information System would also permit digital map data to be displayed graphically. For example, a map image of a city could be displayed on an output station screen and the location of various events within that city portrayed. Digital data describing accidents, welfare cases, school children, residences, new buildings, fires, or civil defense facilities would be shown by type and location in the city. A manager could thus have a periodic photographic location record of environmental events affecting the jurisdiction for which he has a functional responsibility. This graphic representation of digital data would be particularly useful in making management planning and control decisions.

CHAPTER SEVEN

THE UNIFIED INFORMATION SYSTEM:
COSTS AND BENEFITS

COSTS OF THE UNIFIED INFORMATION SYSTEM

The cost of the Unified Information System within any particular state will depend on three major factors: (1) the number of persons and real property parcels in the state; (2) the number, nature, and geographic dispersion of participating governmental units (state agencies, counties, cities, townships, districts, and the constituent departments of each); and (3) the required data processing equipment and facilities.

Determining the number of persons and parcels in a state is relatively straightforward. The approximate numbers are known for the present and can be reasonably estimated for the 1970-75 period.

Estimating the number of governmental units within a state that would participate in such a system is more difficult. The total number of units in each state is known from the *Census of Governments*; but the number of participants and the extent of participation in a Unified Information System would depend on several factors. First, because the System deals with data of primary concern to state, county, and city agencies, it is likely that only a small proportion of the numerous districts would be directly connected into the System. Districts and other units of government not connected directly by electrical or other automatic terminal devices could, of course, both submit inquiries and data and receive output by mail. Second, the size of the governmental unit and of the constituent departments of large units, would affect participation. A small rural county, for example, would neither generate many data for storage and processing in the System nor require frequent or rapid access to data in the Information Center files. The input and output that would be required by such small units could often be handled by a combination of mail and inexpensive inquiry devices. Third, the governmental unit's functions and environment would be important. Some functions—for example, law enforcement, assessment, zoning, and welfare—demand extensive data handling. Others—for example, recreation, animal regulation, and sanitation—require less. Furthermore, since urban areas would normally generate more data than rural areas, units with responsibilities in the former would doubtless participate more extensively in the System. Estimates of the number of participating agencies and the extent of their participation should take these three factors into account as well as the trends and prospects in state and local governments discussed earlier.

The final major factor in determining the over-all cost of the Unified Information System in a state will be the costs of required data handling equipment and facilities. Since the Unified Information System is designed for the 1970-75 period, hardware costs for that period can only be estimated. They will depend on many factors, including inflation, that cannot be predicted precisely. The following discussion of cost is, we believe, a reasonable approach to cost characteristics. In general, we have based estimates on the trends in existing or known hardware and techniques, after extensive discussions with equipment manufacturers and research specialists. The estimates assume no major unforeseen technological breakthroughs that would significantly reduce equipment costs. If such breakthroughs occur, they will further lower the costs of the Unified Information System.

Equipment costs can be associated with the five phases of a data handling system—input, output, communication, storage, and processing—as well as the costs of system programming and operation and Information Center facilities.

Input/Output/Inquiry

In the Unified Information System, input, output, and inquiries are handled by stations located in governmental units. Such stations would have differing capabilities, depending on the requirements of the user. For example, one device to read documents optically might suffice for a city of 100,000, but several other devices for inquiry or output in different departments of the city might be required. Punch cards and punched paper tape will remain major media for input to the system. Devices for receiving data in these forms will be particularly attractive to agencies with insufficient input volume to justify the more expensive optical readers. Often, cards and tape will be automatically created as byproduct records resulting from the operation of equipment located in the various agencies; they will provide semiautomatic input to the Center.

Inquiry stations will be frequently employed; keyboard input and printed output will be used for communication between agencies and the Center.

Such devices will be inexpensive and can be located in several departments of a governmental unit to facilitate such inquiries as property ownership, zoning or land use, and person identification and background. High speed, large volume printing devices for preparing tax bills, licenses, and precinct lists could be centrally located to serve all departments of an agency. Similarly, display devices could serve an entire governmental unit. Agencies can, of course, share the more expensive devices, especially optical readers, high capacity printers, and display devices.

Costs will vary according to equipment capability. The following unit costs are ranges for presently available equipment classes and are approximations for the 1970-75 period. Annual cost is the annual rental cost in 1963 dollars. (Equipment purchase prices are generally about four to five times annual rental cost.)

	Present Annual Cost	1970–75 Estimated Annual Cost
Optical reading station	$30,000–36,000	$8,000–12,000
Punch card/paper tape station	1,500– 1,800	1,000– 1,500
Keyboard inquiry station	180– 3,000	150– 600
High capacity printer	9,000–24,000	8,000–12,000
Display device	8,000–30,000	8,000–12,000

Substantial declines in costs for optical readers and inquiry stations are predicated on intensive research now underway on these devices and on the large potential market that should make volume production possible. Cost reductions may also be expected in display devices and, to a lesser extent, in printers and card/tape readers.

Communications

Communications costs are attributable to terminal equipment and to message transmissions. In the Unified Information System, terminal equipment links input/output/inquiry stations to the common carrier communications network. The cost of such terminal equipment is related to transmission capacity. The following figures are estimates for both high capacity devices (for bulk data transmission) and lower capacity devices (for inquiries and responses).

	Present Annual Cost	1970–75 Estimated Annual Cost
High capacity: several hundred characters per second	$1500–6000	$1000–1500
Low capacity: fifteen to one hundred characters per second	200–1500	100– 200

Terminal equipment costs can be expected to decline because of technological advances and volume production.

Transmission costs depend primarily on the amount of time the circuits are used and the distance between the Center and the remote stations. *Intra*state transmission costs promise to decline substantially during the 1960's, just as *inter*state rates have declined in recent years. Wide area service, Telpak, full-time leased channels, and the dial-up message network all appear economically and technically attractive for the Unified Information System. The particular configuration of circuits in each state would have to be determined individually, depending on distances between the Center and all remote stations and the message volumes. Many messages in the Unified Information System, such as data sent from agencies to update Center files and data sent to agencies for extensive printed output, could be transmitted during night hours on regular message circuits at lower rates. Also, governmental units could jointly lease full-time circuits. Because of the high speed of character transmission (already up to 300 characters per second by conventional common-carrier message facilities), no significant delay would be entailed by use of joint circuits. As a conservative estimate of transmission costs, we can calculate the cost of connecting all participating government agencies with the Center by full-time leased circuits. Such circuits would be available full time for data transmission and could be shared by several agencies, depending on message volume. This method, and the circuit cost of $36 per mile per year, provides a reasonable estimate of transmission expenses within a state even though a mix of services would undoubtedly be used. This mileage cost approximates present *inter*state charges, and telephone company representatives have estimated that *intra*state rates will drop to this range during the decade.

Storage

The cost per character of storing data in large, rapid access files has steadily declined, until today it is about one-third of what it was five years ago. Current large volume disc storage devices are available in the range of $0.0006 to $0.0008 per character per year. It appears that the technology of magnetic storage will continue to advance and that the cost for large files will decline by 1970-75 to the approximate range of $0.0001 to $0.0003 per year per character stored. Technological breakthroughs in both magnetic and nonmagnetic storage may reduce the unit cost even further.

Processing

Because most state and local government functions entail relatively simple and straightforward data processing, the computing capability required in the Unified Information System could generally be met by equipment available today. Today's costs for processing capability are likely to diminish somewhat, though relatively less than declines in communications and storage costs. It is reasonable to expect that sufficient processing capability for the Information Center facilities of a typical state will be available in the early 1970's for an annual rental in the range of $600,000 to $1,200,000, including communications switching hardware located at the Center. These sums should provide a processing capability several times that offered by current equipment costing in this range.

Other Costs

Costs of the Unified Information System, except those identified above, would be associated mainly with the operation of the Information Center. Programming the System would undoubtedly be a gradual process following the steps toward implementation outlined in Chapter 8. Annual costs directly attributable to detailed system analysis, programming, and operations in most states would be in the range of $1,500,000 to $3,000,000 per year, or about 100 to 200 men at $15,000 each. This manpower estimate is based on several recent large scale data system efforts, including nation-wide airline reservation systems and world-wide military inventory control and air defense systems. The cost is based on projection of current salaries and related costs of about $11,000 per man-year to estimated 1970 levels.

Physical facilities to house the Center equipment and personnel would require a one-time expenditure ranging from $625,000 to $1,250,000 (25,000 to 50,000 square feet at $25 per square foot). This can be divided by twenty-five years to estimate an annual facility cost. In summary form, Unified Information System unit costs for the 1970-75 period are estimated as follows:

Item	Range of Estimated Annual Costs
Input/output/inquiry	
Optical reading station	$ 8,000–12,000
Punch card/paper tape station	1,000– 1,500
Keyboard inquiry station	150– 600
High capacity printer	8,000–12,000
Display device	8,000–12,000
Communications	
Terminal equipment	
High capacity	1,000– 1,500
Low capacity	100– 200
Transmission	36 per mile
Storage, per character stored	0.0001–0.0003

Processing $600,000–1,200,000

Other:

Programming and operations 1,500,000–3,000,000

Physical Center facilities
(one-time, $625,000–1,250,000) 25,000–   50,000

These estimated unit costs are sensitive to different factors within each state. Input/output/inquiry and communications costs are related directly to the number of remote stations in the System and are, therefore, highly variable. Processing and programming costs, on the other hand, are much less variable because of the large fixed cost of having *any* computer and *any* system.

To estimate how actual costs might develop, we have selected for analysis five states of markedly differing location, population, area, and government organization. Table 7 shows the cost analysis, which is further explained below. Costs for other states can reasonably be estimated by the same method. Persons (line 1) and parcels (line 2) are known for the years indicated, and the number of characters stored (line 3) is based on the formula described in the discussion of *storage* in Chapter 6. It should be noted that *doubling* the number of characters (to allow for population and parcel growth, a street section file, or storage of additional data) increases total system costs by only the following percentage in each state: California, 7.8; Michigan, 7.1; Nebraska, 2.4; New Hampshire, 1.4; Virginia, 6.6. Governmental units (lines 4-10) are known. The estimated number of remote terminal connections (line 11) is based on a careful analysis of the following primary factors in each state: area and population of the entire state and its local political subdivisions; number of governmental units and their nature—for example, school districts are small in Nebraska and large in Virginia; and the urban-rural character of the state and its political subdivisions. Based on this analysis, an estimate was made of the probable participation of government agencies and their departments and the remote stations of all types that would be required. In Table 7 and the discussion below, the costs are based on this estimate and the estimated unit costs of data handling equipment and facilities.

The costs for each state are generally calculated from the midpoints of the cost ranges given earlier. Where the characteristics of the state or of the devices required are unusual, the midpoint estimation method is appropriately modified. For example, maximum processing costs are used for California because it is a large state requiring a large capacity system.

Input/output/inquiry (line 12) and communication terminal costs (line 13) vary according to the remote stations connected. Communications transmission costs (line 14) are based on the size of each state and

TABLE 7

ESTIMATED COST IN FIVE STATES FOR A UNIFIED INFORMATION SYSTEM

Line No.	Item	California	Michigan	Nebraska	New Hampshire	Virginia
1	Persons (1960)	15,717,204	7,823,194	1,411,330	606,921	3,966,949
2	Parcels (1961)	5,501,000	3,136,000	696,000	267,000	1,545,000
3	Estimated characters stored	5,469,450,000	2,841,870,000	551,700,000	227,520,000	1,427,400,000
4	Government units (1962)	4,023	3,817	5,125	551	381
5	State	1	1	1	1	1
6	County	57	83	93	10	98
7	City	373	509	537	13	236
8	Township	...	1,259	478	221	...
9	Special District	1,962	99	752	85	46
10	School District	1,630	1,866	3,264	221	...
11	Estimated remote terminal connections of all kinds to governmental agencies	3,390	1,877	1,372	347	671
12	Estimated annual costs: Input/output/inquiry	$ 5,388,000	$3,038,000	$1,359,000	$ 870,000	$1,210,000
	Communications					
13	Terminals	1,205,000	649,000	383,000	161,000	249,000
14	Transmission	2,030,000	677,000	497,000	32,000	122,000
15	Storage	1,094,000	568,000	110,000	46,000	285,000
16	Processing	1,200,000	1,000,000	800,000	600,000	900,000
	Other					
17	Programming, operations	3,000,000	2,000,000	1,500,000	1,500,000	1,500,000
18	Facilities	46,000	36,000	26,000	26,000	26,000
19	Total estimated annual costs	$13,963,000	$7,968,000	$4,675,000	$3,235,000	$4,292,000

the number of remote stations. Storage costs (line 15) are calculated by multiplying the number of characters to be stored by the average unit cost of $0.0002. Processing cost (line 16) is a lump-sum amount based on the estimated computing capability required at the Information Center. Programming and operations (line 17) represents the estimated number of annual man-years multiplied by $15,000. Facilities cost (line 18) is based on the estimated amount of space required for the Information Center.

In evaluating these estimated costs of the Unified Information System, it would be helpful to know the cost of present methods of handling the data. Such costs are difficult to identify because data processing is seldom an expenditure classification in government accounts. However, data processing costs are a sizable factor in state and local government expenditures. Administrators in each state are best qualified to judge their own present data processing costs.

For the five states discussed above, total expenditures of state and local governments in 1960 are given in Table 8. Also shown are the estimated costs of the Unified Information System in each state and the percentage of total expenditures these costs comprise.

TABLE 8

UNIFIED INFORMATION SYSTEM COSTS COMPARED WITH
TOTAL EXPENDITURES IN FIVE STATES

State	State and Local Government Expenditures (1960)	Estimated Unified Information System Costs	System-Cost Percentage of Expenditures
California	$6,021,000,000	$13,963,000	0.23%
Michigan	2,372,000,000	7,968,000	0.34%
Nebraska	380,000,000	4,675,000	1.23%
New Hampshire	168,000,000	3,235,000	1.93%
Virginia	848,000,000	4,292,000	0.51%

Detailed analyses should be made for each state of both current data handling costs and the costs of the proposed system. These costs can then be measured against the values and benefits of the Unified Information System outlined in the following section. We believe that the result will be emphatic corroboration of the over-all, long-run economies and advantages of the Unified Information System.

Since the System serves a complex of governmental units in a state, the estimated cost to each participating unit is of interest. This cost would depend principally on (1) the number and nature of input/output/inquiry stations and communications terminals located in the unit; (2) communications transmission costs based on use of circuit facilities—similar to present telephone methods; (3) direct cost of programming and processing done for the unit by the Information Center; and (4) a pro rata share of Information Center costs, such as storage, general programming, facilities, and processing, based on the proportional number of persons and parcels in the unit's jurisdiction.

In conclusion, we emphasize that this cost exercise has been designed to reveal the *general range of costs* for the Unified Information System within a state during the 1970-75 period. These costs are low, when weighed against the System's benefits and against the major alternative approach of data systems and equipment configurations limited to individual agencies and departments. At some points the Unified Information System may be more costly than a more limited system, but when total data handling costs of performing government functions are considered and the values of more accessible, more accurate, and more usable information are fully assessed, the Unified Information System appears to be economically attractive as well as technologically and administratively feasible.

BENEFITS OF THE UNIFIED INFORMATION SYSTEM

System benefits may be considered in relation to the System objectives outlined earlier: reducing duplication in data collection, storage, and processing, and increasing the accessibility and usefulness of data. Both types of benefits can lead, in turn, to lower costs in information handling itself and to improvements in the management decision-making of participating agencies.

Reduction of Duplication

We have pointed out the extensive duplication that currently exists in collecting, storing, and processing data items for government functions; much of this duplication would be eliminated by the Unified Information System.

First, a state-wide central file of data describing persons and parcels would supersede many files kept by units and departments. Several of these existing files are very large, containing millions of characters; others are small but costly to maintain. The following major files would be good candidates for dissolution once the data they contain were made part of the Unified files:

Persons

Unemployment insurance
Licensing of all kinds, especially drivers' and vocational licenses

Voters' registration
Juror selection
Income tax
Criminal identification
Outstanding warrants
Welfare assistance, including the "confidential index"
Vital statistics

Parcels

Property assessing
Planning, especially land use and zoning
Tax delinquency
Vacant property
Location files of many functions, such as licensing, fire, police, health, agriculture, refuse collection, building construction, revenue
Special assessment districts

We again emphasize that dissolution of these files need not degrade the performance of any function or the integrity of any department. Only the data used to perform the functions would be affected, and they would be made more accessible and usable to the function concerned. Source-documents would continue to remain in the functional departments; only the data from these documents would enter the Unified Information System.

Second, the Unified Information System would permit the discontinuance of many individual agency input systems as a more comprehensive input system to serve all units was implemented. In particular, functions could less often use their own field personnel to gather data if the aims and methods discussed earlier about input were executed. Since semiautomatic inquiries for data could be made by citizens directly to the Information Center, agencies could also assign fewer employees for providing person and parcel information to the public.

Significant cost savings in each agency's data handling would undoubtedly result from the reduction of duplication. Such savings would not be expected for several years, however, since many agencies would carry on parallel operations during the early phases of implementing the System. They would continue parallel operations because of their understandable reluctance to abandon their present systems until they were certain of the reliability of the Unified Information System. Increased cost can be expected during this period of parallel operation, but in the long run the over-all savings should be significant.

Increase in Accessibility and Usefulness of Information

We believe that the System's greatest benefits lie in increasing the accessibility and usefulness of data.

In the first place, comprehensive current information about a person or parcel would be easily accessible. More functions are asking for greater volumes of data on individual and aggregate persons and parcels. Let us first consider some typical uses and benefits of the comprehensive data available in the System files about persons.

Person Data. Verification: Agencies often need to verify a person's identity, address, marital status, and similar data. At present, they send out verification letters to as many other agencies as they believe may have relevant information. For example, in verifying the background of an applicant for welfare assistance, the following agencies are typically contacted: local police, state bureau of criminal identification, school district attended by the applicant, department of employment, registrar of voters, county assessor, veterans' office, bureau of vocational rehabilitation, office of vital statistics, probation department, county clerk's office, and department of motor vehicles. Having all such data available from a single source would greatly ease the burden of this work.

In addition, all changes in a particular person's status would automatically be available to any interested agency. Thus, for example, when a change of address was reported to the department of motor vehicles, the correct address for that person would be recorded in the System file and would be available to all interested agencies. Similarly, changes in marital status and other identifying characteristics, as well as items we have described as status data, would be updated and currently maintained within the System.

Notification: When particular events happen to persons, certain government agencies are interested. For example, in California, when a person dies in a home for the aged that is under the jurisdiction of a public agency, state law requires that the state Department of Social Welfare be notified within forty-eight hours. Under present systems, a death certificate is filed and separate notification is sent to the Department of Social Welfare. Under the Unified Information System, the filing of the death certificate itself would automatically both notify all interested departments of this event and record relevant data describing the event in the System file for the person concerned. Similarly, persons whose whereabouts are of concern to law enforcement agencies would have their current addresses maintained in the System, and address changes reported to any agency would trigger the automatic notification of all other interested agencies. Some governmental units would require overt notice, whereas others would be satisfied with the currency of the data on file which could be interrogated as needed.

Outstanding Warrants: At any given time thousands of warrants for the arrest of persons for both major and minor offenses are outstanding. Police departments lack the manpower to send officers looking for all such persons, many of whom have been involved in only relatively unimportant traffic violations. Most of the data on a warrant relate to the identity of the person involved and to the characteristics of the warrant itself. Within the Unified Information System, data concerning all outstanding warrants could be filed under the name of the person against whom they were issued. Any transaction affecting that person could be programmed to initiate automatically a report of the existence of outstanding warrants to the proper authorities, and their service upon the involved person would, therefore, be expedited considerably. It would also be possible to program the System so that drivers' licenses would not be issued to persons for whom traffic violation warrants were outstanding until the warrants were cleared. Likewise, registration of vehicles involved in traffic violations could be automatically delayed pending clearance of any outstanding warrants. The revenue resulting directly from such central warrant data would be considerable, and the mechanics of including it within the Unified Information System would be simple.

Licensing: Many government agencies use licenses as a primary device to carry out their regulatory responsibilities. The items of information on a license, whether it authorizes driving automobiles, practicing medicine, or selling machine guns at retail, primarily involve identity data describing the licensee and items describing the authority granted him by the license and the date that this authority expires. Since many citizens carry more than one license, identity data are frequently duplicated; in fact, there are dozens of government license files in which 80 to 90 per cent of the information items are identical.

Within the Unified Information System, many licenses could simply be issued by the System, and records concerning them maintained within the System. Renewal processing, together with notification to interested agencies when any event affecting the licensee occurred, could then be handled automatically.

It should be emphasized that if licenses were issued through and maintained within the Unified Information System, the authority of the agency responsible for the regulation involving the license would in no way be diminished. The System's function would simply be to expedite the data handling involved. The advantages that such a System provides in licensing will no doubt become even more important, since there appears to be a trend toward an increase in the number of kinds of licenses.

Welfare: Considerable recent research about the recipients of various forms of welfare services indicates that many of the families who receive welfare support, such as aid to needy children, are, for example, concurrently receiving attention from the probation department because of juvenile misbehavior, from public hospitals because of the physical needs of destitute members of the family, and from the department of corrections, which has the former breadwinner in custody on a burglary conviction. Several serious proposals have recently been made that social services to so-called problem families should be better coordinated so that, for instance, if one agency is giving money to a destitute family for food, another is not giving this family food baskets to satisfy the same needs. Research on the causes of difficulties that certain families seem to experience would also be facilitated by a more integrated approach to the families that receive most public disciplinary and welfare services. Statistics seem to confirm that a small portion of the population receives a large proportion of the total public welfare services rendered by state and local government agencies. As social services expand and increasing interest is exhibited in an integrated approach to problem families, the usefulness of the Unified Information System in describing the contacts of such families with government agencies becomes increasingly apparent. Indeed, steps toward a Unified Information System would be an almost essential prerequisite to economically undertaking a comprehensive approach to the problem family.

Voters' Registration: As in licensing, voters' registration involves, almost entirely, identity data, plus one or two such items as the voter's political affiliation and his voting precinct. Once the basic data about a person were available in a Unified Information System, adding these specialized items would be simple. As already discussed under "verification" and "notification," the change of a citizen's address could be automatically processed by the System, and, for example, a notice sent to him that because of his new address, he must reregister to vote. Likewise, the file of registered voters could be automatically purged of nonvoters, based on the input of persons who failed to vote at general elections. The first operation—reregistration notice—is not feasible under present manual systems, and the second—purging the Great Register—is today time consuming and costly. Both of these applications would be simple and automatic within the Unified Information System.

Research: As social scientists pursue their research about the behavior of persons, they would be greatly aided by having available within a Unified Information System all basic data about persons. Analyses and correlations presently not possible because of the lack of accessible data would become relatively simple. Furthermore, the data would be kept up to date by automatic and semiautomatic input from the events with which government agencies have routine concern: births, licenses, arrests, employment earnings, welfare payments, school attendance, etc.

The Unified Information System provides for the filing of such data to facilitate intercommunication between all segments in the System; therefore, data about any person or group of persons could easily be extracted from the System regardless of the function or agency originally responsible for collecting the data or primarily concerned with their use. Thus the System would both satisfy the requirements for legal recordkeeping and make feasible important uses for information that presently are not possible.

Real Property Data. Functions interested in real property data would similarly benefit from the comprehensiveness of the Unified Information System central file. Such items as property ownership and land use would be more accessible and accurate than present systems permit. Access to the range of items listed in Chapter 4 dealing with real property might also, for example, permit better decisions to be made in assigning assessed values by providing more data in a form that makes analysis relatively simple. Comprehensive land-use planning, economic base studies, and planning for functional services, such as parks, recreation, transportation, and education, would also have available, in a usable form, volumes of data with which to forecast and program. By providing a current file of such data, the Unified Information System substantially reduces the need for expensive, one-time, data collection programs that are typical of current planning and transportation studies.

Furthermore, the Unified Information System provides a means for co-ordinating the planning programs of various agencies. Plans affecting real property particularly require coordination. Within the System, as soon as an agency has adopted, or is considering adoption of, any plans affecting a parcel or group of parcels, this fact can be reported to the Information Center. It would be recorded in the file as a feature of the parcels affected, and all agencies with an interest in what happens to each parcel would be automatically notified. For example, a plan to redevelop a group of city blocks can be of concern to police, fire, health, water, transportation, school, recreation, structural regulation, welfare, public works, licensing, and revenue functions. Similarly, street widenings and public land acquisitions are of multiple interest. Within the Unified Information System, a report to the Center by the agency proposing such action would permit the automatic notification of other interested agencies early in the planning process. Such comprehensive notification would reduce cases in which, for example, a flood control district, a school board, and a park department—each independently and in ignorance of the plans of the others—would plan to acquire and develop the same parcel for its own use. The comprehensiveness of the Unified Information System would therefore result in improved coordination among government agencies.

The System also would provide a comprehensive file for recording the location of objects and events of government interest. The location of certain of these objects and events concerns nearly every function of government. Many departments now maintain location files; some do not but would like to have data in such form. The real property parcel record provides the vehicle for a common location file for all functions. Such a file would make it possible to record by parcel all data items listed about real property in Chapter 4, as well as specialized data items of interest to single departments. The location of all scales, elevators, and fire extinguishers requiring inspection would be readily available for retrieval and analysis, as well as the location of fires, industrial accidents, crimes, and the places where bad sanitary conditions exist.

Such a location file would also be useful for determining the cost of government services by area. If reports of government services rendered—fire and police calls, welfare visits, health services, assessing inspections, and agricultural visits—were regularly entered onto the records of the parcels affected, the data could easily be aggregated by administrative area or jurisdiction. From a comprehensive record of such services by the location where rendered, responsible government departments could analyze the causes and total costs of their functions by area. Using the parcel as a basic recording unit would permit data to be aggregated according to the boundaries of each jurisdiction concerned. Comprehensive information about environment characteristics by location would also be of value to many functions concerned primarily with services to persons. Parole agencies, educators, and social welfare and public health specialists are all increasingly concerned about the effect of environment on their specific clientele. By providing a comprehensive record of all aspects of this environment, the Unified Information System would provide the base for extensive ecological research and planning.

In addition to the benefits arising from greater comprehensiveness of data, the System would provide several other advantages over separate nonintegrated data systems.

First, automatic checking of data compatibility would be possible. Such checks would compare new information on a person or parcel with information already on file in the System. For example, if a report were received that application had been made to open a restaurant-cocktail lounge at a particular location, the computer could make an automatic check to verify that the property was zoned for that type of operation and that *all* permits required had been applied for and granted (health, alcoholic beverage, sales tax, etc.). This automatic check could save many hours of manual review required to make the same determination. With respect to persons, if someone applied for relief funds, the computer could automatically check to see if he were gainfully employed, what his prior earnings were, and whether he owned property in excess of an allowable maximum. After this "compatibility search," the appropriate departments could be automatically notified. Such searches could also be made to ensure the proper payment of taxes levied by different agencies on the same person.

Second, data entering the System could be automatically monitored for unusual conditions and for statistical reporting. Events often become significant for action upon accumulation, for example, a third fire at a single location, or a person's repeated application for public assistance in different counties. The System would provide a means for detecting such accumulated events in accordance with rules prescribed by the participating agencies. The computer could simply tally events described by data reported to it and report as directed when a specified norm was exceeded. Statistical data about the numbers of events of interest to each participating agency could also be automatically accumulated and regularly reported in aggregate.

Third, the System would enable automatic searches to be made for persons or parcels with specified characteristics, apart from name or specific address. For example, an industrial promotion agency might wish to locate a parcel in a general area with the following characteristics: ten-acre size, zoning for light industry, access to secondary highway, and access to utilities; or a law enforcement agency, knowing the physical characteristics of a suspect, might wish to discover his identity. In these and other similar cases, the Unified Information System could automatically search its files and produce lists of parcels and persons having the specified characteristics.

Fourth, the Unified Information System would vastly improve access to the information required for the use of many of the newer, so-called scientific tools of management, such as simulation and linear programming. These tools are heavily dependent on data and are often costly to use if extensive original data collection is required. By providing comprehensive files of data in accessible form, the System would make the use of mathematical models and quantitative tools economically attractive. It also would provide a powerful computing facility to manipulate the data in accordance with the complex formulae such tools typically involve.

Stability of Organization Environment

Finally, since the Unified Information System deals with individual items of information, and since all information is filed by parcels of land and individual persons, we believe that changes in government organization or in the way data are used to perform functions would cause little disruption of the information-handling system. This is true because the system is designed to capture the basic data as near to their original source as possible and to record them directly in a central file describing the person or parcel affected. They are then available to all agencies having an authorized need. If the responsibility for certain activities were shifted from one agency to another, the data in the System would be just as available to the new agency as to the one having prior responsibility. Transfers of authority and responsibility would therefore involve a minimum of conversion problems and resulting confusion in the transfer of the data. This advantage results from the fact that the System is designed with little regard to those who actually collect, store, and use the data, but rather is built around the data items themselves and the objects they describe. This characteristic would also provide maximum flexibility in supplying authorized data to private citizens, firms, and Federal agencies. Similarly, it would facilitate the combining of data from private or Federal government sources with the person and parcel data within the System.

CHAPTER EIGHT

STEPS TOWARD IMPLEMENTATION

The Unified Information System is a long-range goal designed to employ the EDP equipment capability that will be available in the early 1970's. During the 1960's, state and local governments will and should develop data systems to serve their own requirements. These systems will use existing data processing equipment and should be designed both to serve the particular needs of the agency concerned and to fit logically into the future Unified Information System. Carefully designed individual systems will offer significant benefits in themselves and provide many of the steps leading toward the Unified System. This chapter discusses the design of these systems and outlines the steps leading toward implementation of the Unified Information System for state and local governments.

ACTION BY INDIVIDUAL GOVERNMENTAL UNITS

We believe current data systems designed individually by governmental units should be patterned after the Unified Information System described in Chapters 5, 6, and 7. Although many of the benefits of the Unified Information System derive from its *inter*governmental nature, its approach and concept are directly relevant to systems limited to single units. Such *intra*governmental data systems should be designed as microcosms or miniatures of the Unified Information System in all respects. Almost everything discussed earlier about input, output, communications, storage, and processing, as well as the question of centralization and the role of the Information Center in a state-wide system, can be scaled down in scope and applied to the data system of individual governmental units.

In pursuing this objective, governmental units should observe the following principles:

1. *Make the system comprehensive within the governmental unit.* Data systems should not be confined to a single functional department in their

scope because most data are not limited to a single function in their use. The system should therefore serve an entire governmental unit, not merely one or more of its functional departments. Only through this approach can the system both reduce duplication in data collection and storage and increase the accessibility and usefulness of data. This is a basic principle that should pervade the design of data systems by governmental units from initial analysis to final implementation.

2. *Establish central data files within the unit by person and/or parcel,[1] not by function or department.* All the rationale for filing by these categories in the United Information System applies equally to systems for individual governmental units. Such files suggest each unit's creation of an organizational "Information Center" like that of the Unified Information System. Because of the limited size of most governmental units (except for larger states, counties, and cities), such an Information Center would often possess the only extensive data handling equipment within the unit. It would, therefore, often perform *all* the mechanized data handling of both common and specialized environmental data, as well as internal operating information about the unit. In handling specialized departmental data, it would serve primarily as a service bureau for the departments; whereas in handling common data describing persons and parcels, it would be the focal point of an integrated data system for the entire unit. We believe the unit's major effort should go toward establishing jurisdiction-wide files of data by person and parcel. Creation of data systems built around persons and parcels would take priority over automating single applications, such as voters' registration, tax billing, or crop statistics. These types of applications would be performed using appropriate data from the person or property files once these files and the systems serving them were established. Secondary efforts should generally be given to dealing with specialized data of unique interest within a single functional department.

3. *Conduct inventories of data items within all department files from the person- and/or parcel-category viewpoint.* Such inventories can begin with an analysis of the forms used by the departments, and should document the source and disposition of each data item on every form. Completed, rather than blank, forms should be analyzed to determine actual data-use patterns. Throughout the form analysis, focus should be not on the forms themselves but on the items of information they convey. Forms can then be redesigned in accordance with the requirements of the revised data system.

Extensive interviews are also necessary to identify all the data items used in a particular function. Such interviews should similarly focus on specific

---

[1] The term "parcel" includes street sections, which would constitute a separate real property file.

data items, their source, and disposition. Data which could be used but are not presently available should also be identified for each organizational element so that the revised system can be designed to supply them.

This data item inventory can be facilitated by using the item listings in Chapter 4. Because these listings were derived from an analysis of the entire range of state and local governments, they are considerably more extensive than they would be for any single governmental unit. For example, our real property file for parcels lists well over 100 items; a similar file proposed for a city of 35,000 population included 42 of these items. Because of their inclusiveness, our listings provide a comprehensive guide to the kind and range of items that each governmental unit can look for within its own departments.

Such an inventory of data items invariably will lead to the discovery of many inaccuracies and inconsistencies within existing data systems. Conflicting data definitions, incorrect data recording, and great gaps in the information "everyone is certain existed" will be uncovered. A beneficial byproduct of the data item inventory is the opportunity to correct these data deficiencies prior to installing the improved system.

The end product of the data item inventory is a master listing of the items to be included within the central person and/or parcel files of the governmental unit. This master listing should include, for each item, the number of characters required, the source (department and form), and the functions in which it is used.

4. *Develop uniform object identification systems.* Uniform systems for identifying persons, parcels, and street sections are essential both for handling data that are part of the common files and for interrelating common and specialized data. Uniform object identification thus permits the merging of data from several files, such as common parcel data with specialized data from the files of utility, schools, agriculture, and licensing functions. Such uniform systems should be as comprehensive as possible, ideally extending across many governmental units, especially local agencies in the same urban area. Interagency standardization of object identification systems is essential if incompatible systems are to be avoided; it should be accomplished at the earliest possible stage in the system design. Where metropolitan areas transcend state boundaries, efforts should be made to develop systems that are compatible among all affected states.

Parcel numbers for real property should be assigned systematically. Several parcel numbering systems are in use, the better ones relating parcel numbers to a map depicting the parcel described. Frequently, the parcel number used to identify property for tax assessment can be adopted or modified for use in the central parcel file.

Street section codes should be developed by governmental units dealing with any data describing characteristics of public rights of way. Such section codes are currently common in larger traffic and road departments. Because streets often run through several governmental units, cooperative efforts by all affected units are desirable.

Grid systems should be designed for identifying and aggregating real property apart from political, geographic, and topographic indicators. Partial grid systems exist in nearly every part of the country, but most are incomplete in their coverage or too gross in their precision. Basic state-wide systems should be adopted that allow for local modifications to fit the needs of local agencies. The degree of precision and detail furnished by a grid system within each local jurisdiction is a matter for that jurisdiction to determine for itself.

Social Security numbers should be used for identification on all input documents containing data about persons. They are distinctly the most suitable identifiers; and even though they may not be needed immediately in every case, they should be included on input documents so that people will become accustomed to recording them. Uniform numbers to identify all firms about which data are kept are equally important. They can be generated by any appropriate agency and should then be used by all agencies.

5. *Design the data system, and especially the person and/or parcel files, for use in regular operations of the governmental unit concerned.* In particular, the central person and parcel files should not simply be *additional* files—they should *replace* files in several functional departments. This procedure can yield direct money savings, while the continuance of redundant department files will inevitably increase costs.

We stress this point because there appears to be a nation-wide trend, especially in local planning departments, to establish limited parcel files containing data gathered from several departments. Nowhere have we seen any interest in dissolving the files in the departments from which the "planning" data are gathered. Rather, it seems only that an additional central file is created. This is generally a result of insufficient attention to designing a comprehensive data system to serve the entire governmental unit. It is highly preferable to spend more time on the design of a system using a central parcel file in the regular operations of the several departments which gather the data than to perpetuate parallelism and duplication by simply creating additional files. As in the Unified Information System, data from this central file would be available to various departments.

No reduction in department function or integrity is entailed by central person and/or parcel files. Only data items are affected, and they are made more useful than department systems alone would permit. Some larger departments might, of course, continue to maintain specialized data files, some mechanized and some manual. Dividing data items between common and specialized files would follow the same rules described in our discussion of the Unified Information System. In every case, the use to which the individual data items are put would govern in each phase of the data system design.

6. *Consider file consolidation within the person and parcel categories by grafting additional items of data onto existing major files.* Within state and local governments, several major files already exist by person and parcel: *person*—licensing, voters' registration, taxation, and employment insurance; *parcel*—tax assessing, property ownership, utility, fire inspection, zoning and land use, and improvement districts.

In some cases, cities, counties, and state governments may find it beneficial to expand the number of data items in one of these files by adding to it items from other files, which then could be dissolved. For the person file, any of the files above would provide a good beginning; for the parcel file, property assessment records seem particularly appropriate because of their comprehensiveness. If this is done, the resulting file of items probably should assume the designation of "person" or "parcel" rather than that of the function whose file has been expanded. It may also be desirable to establish the new file in the local agency's "Information Center" rather than to continue it within the management jurisdiction of a single functional department. Such decisions depend primarily on the particulars of the organization involved.

7. *Expand the data collection responsibilities of various department field personnel.* Everything in our discussion of input to the Unified Information System applies equally well to a system for a single governmental unit. In particular, field personnel of all departments should be considered as potential collectors of data for use by departments other than the one for which they work. Firemen on periodic fire prevention inspections, license inspectors, utility personnel, social welfare field workers, and building inspectors can all be excellent data collectors for cities and counties.

Design of citizen-initiated input documents from a comprehensive viewpoint, as discussed in describing the Unified Information System, can also lead both to direct economies and to improved citizen-relations.

8. *Use existing data processing equipment capability.* Many state and local governments can profitably employ existing data processing equipment. Use of currently available equipment is discussed in Appendix B.

It should be pointed out that the data system principles outlined here pertain to government agencies of all sizes; they do not require that an agency be large enough to afford its own equipment. These principles apply equally to small and large organizations, and would result in substantial data *system* improvements regardless of whether electronic computers, punch card devices, or manual systems were employed. Therefore we emphasize that all state and local governmental units should begin making data system improvements in accordance with these principles.

TRANSITION TO THE UNIFIED INFORMATION SYSTEM

The first step toward implementing the Unified Information System for state and local governments is to establish microcosms of the Unified Information System in these units. This step will take several years. Toward the end of the 1960's, we believe, the parallelism among these several unit systems will become evident. For example, cities will become aware of the parallelism between their real property files and the similar file of the county in which the cities are located. Likewise, person files developed by counties and state governments will reveal duplications. At this point the Unified Information System will become particularly attractive.

For local agencies—cities, counties, townships, and districts—and decentralized regions of state departments, the concept of a regional version of the ultimate state-wide system appears interesting and feasible as a transition step. In particular, local agencies in the same urban metropolitan area may find this approach useful. Such regional systems are especially attractive for data describing real property. Regional systems could be sponsored cooperatively by a number of governmental units or provided as a service by a unit with broad geographic jurisdiction in a region, such as a county or a group of counties. Again, we stress that we are not describing a conventional service-bureau operation which simply processes client data, but a *system*, structured around information categories of real property and persons, wherein every phase of data handling from input to use is connected by interdependent and comprehensive procedures.

Although regional systems may be desirable as transitional steps to the Unified Information System, the long-range goal should be a state-wide system because of the increasing interactions and interdependencies of state and local agencies within a state and the fact that many of the data used by *local* agencies in a region are, or can be, efficiently collected in the course of normal *state* agency operations, such as employment insurance, licensing, law enforcement, and industrial relations. State agencies similarly have interest in data gathered by such local units as health, education, zoning, structural regulation, law enforcement, and traffic engineering.

Another transition step would be the consolidation of two or more functional files into a single joint file within either the person or real property categories. Just as this can be done *within* an agency, it can be accomplished *between* agencies. (Examples are given in the earlier discussion under principle 6.) Such file consolidation on a more modest basis than that proposed for the ultimate system would involve grafting items of data from two or more agency files onto a common file, after which the predecessor files could be dissolved. Ultimately, such consolidated files could form the basis for the Unified Information System.

In addition to these transitional steps, we believe that agencies and professional associations of government personnel should immediately and cooperatively establish data system study committees such as those now working in industry. Such existing groups include a life-insurance association automation committee, a banking-association automation committee, and similar groups from the air transportation and retail industries. These committees, composed of persons from several companies making up an industry, work on common problems of data system design, particularly those involving the exchange of data among different companies. Since the traditional interrelationships between state and local governmental units are closer and the climate for cooperation warmer than is typical in such industrial groups, the motivation should be even stronger for government agencies and personnel to cooperate in studying this field. Such state and local groups as those currently studying emergency communications and uniform building codes provide precedents for such action.

These committees should include representatives from the several functions of state and local governments as well as from their different levels: city, county, state, township, and district. Professional associations of government personnel should also be represented. Such committees would focus on the data categories of persons and real property; among their functions would be the following:

(a) To discuss and identify data needed to perform the functions of these governmental units and to develop improved procedures for using them. There is a great need to learn more about the use and value of information, especially in management planning and control decisions.

(b) To standardize the meaning of data terms and to develop equivalencies to be used for aggregating data on a comprehensive basis. Data standardization is also necessary to permit the exchange of data between governmental units during transition to the Unified Information System. The need for such research, particularly for terminological equivalencies, was discussed in Chapter 5.

(c) To develop classifications and codifications of data which will reduce storage and increase the facility of use of data items needed by state and local governments. Such classification and codification is a logical step following the standardization of meaning (b).

(d) To work on rules for the inference of certain kinds of data from the existence of other kinds. For example, the issuance of a particular kind of license or the growth of a particular crop may indicate other characteristics of the parcel concerned, such as land use, just as certain events which have happened to persons can indicate probable characteristics of these persons. These inferential relationships are useful in research analysis of data and can lead to considerably greater understanding about the environment in which state and local governments operate. They also facilitate automatic data editing, which increases the accuracy of data within the system.

(e) To encourage the development and adoption of uniform object identification systems. As discussed above under principle 4, the adoption of comprehensive, uniform object identification systems within and especially between agencies is essential both for immediate local systems and for the Unified Information System.

(f) To establish a basis for sharing data processing equipment programs developed by the various participants.

Conclusion

We recognize that the implementation of any system involves considerable compromise to secure acceptance in a particular organizational environment. Our purpose in describing the Unified Information System has been to present a preferred system. Governmental units are urged to keep two central principles in mind as they consider these proposals. *First,* data systems for state and local governments should be designed primarily to serve the objectives of the governmental unit as a whole rather than those of its constituent functional departments as separate entities. *Second,* major environmental data systems for state and local governments should be comprehensively designed around the information categories of persons and real property parcels.

The Unified Information System is presented as a long-range goal for state and local governments because development of large-scale systems requires considerable time. For example, the installation of a large-scale computer system for property tax assessment in an urban county took five years from initial study to regular operation, although it was essentially a job of straightforward conversion from punch card to electronic processing. An airlines reservation system that currently uses extensive automatic data processing equipment has taken a decade from conception to operation.[2] Intensive *systems* work during the 1960's will be required to design and develop the Unified Information System even though sufficient *hard-*

---

[2] For a description of this and another major system development effort involving a combination of centralization and decentralization, see James D. Gallagher, *Management Information Systems and the Computer,* American Management Association, New York, 1961, Chapter 4.

ware capability will be available in the next two to three years. Given the nature of environmental data and the trends in both EDP technology and state and local governments, we are convinced that this System is preferable to each unit's or department's planning, over the long run, to operate a separate, independent system with its own complete set of equipment.

DATA ITEM DESCRIPTIONS

REAL PROPERTY PARCEL RECORD ITEM DEFINITIONS

Locational Information

1. *Parcel number* is an efficient way to identify each parcel of land separately in a system. A parcel is defined as "a contiguous area of land in one ownership and one general use." Developed originally for use by assessors, parcel-numbering systems customarily index every parcel of land to a basic map. The numbers themselves often refer to a map book, page, and specific parcel on that page. As defined by assessors, parcels are usually but not always equivalent to each piece of property with a separate basic legal description. Parcels of publicly owned property should be included in the system although they are usually nontaxable.

2. *Parcel address(es)* provides a second, though less comprehensive and accurate, index to real property parcels. Street addresses are useful in urban areas, but in agricultural, rural, and undeveloped areas, the parcel number is the only simple means of identifying property. Where several addresses apply to the same parcel, each separate address can be indexed to the appropriate parcel number.

3. *Legal description* is a narrative or numerical description of the parcel identified by the parcel number. A legal description can be in the form of "township and section," relating a piece of land to official U.S. government surveys; it can be by "metes and bounds," measured from established reference points in official maps; or it can be by "lot, block, and tract," which references parcels to maps of recorded subdivisions of property. Complete legal descriptions, particularly those using metes and bounds, are often long and complicated and are seldom used except in connection with property titles. The abbreviated legal description identifying each parcel is a means of identifying the basic complete legal descriptions. Such

a basic legal description describes every piece of land as its dimensions have been recorded regardless of present ownership or use.

4. *Grid coordinates* permits locations to be identified apart from political or topographic references. Complete state-wide coordinate systems are unusual today, but partial systems are in effect in several states. The U.S. government range-township system covers all public lands and many areas previously owned by the Federal government; it can be used efficiently to divide land into ten-acre parcels in areas that have been surveyed. Zone coordinate systems, which correct many of the errors in the Federal range-township system, are used in some states, and cadastral surveys are continuously underway. Military grid systems have also been developed and applied in most of the country, and several defense agencies have active mapping programs which use grids. The Federal Office of Defense Mobilization has an extensive nation-wide grid system. Uniform state-wide coordinate systems have been advocated and may eventually evolve in many states.

In the meantime, present systems can be used where they exist. Thus, for every parcel of land there can be recorded the coordinates defining the parcel itself or the quadrangle into which it falls, according to any grid system that has been applied to the area where the parcel is located. Notations could be entered both for detailed grids where they exist and for gross coordinates in areas that have not been precisely surveyed. For many purposes, street sections can be used as grid coordinates. A grid coordinate system can be used primarily to aggregate parcels by area apart from political or jurisdictional codes.

5. *Street section reference* lists the number of any streets or alleys adjacent to the parcel. The side of the street section on which the parcel lies could be appended to the reference number. Data items filed by street section are discussed on p. 117.

6. *Parcel numbers of adjacent parcels* is self-explanatory.

7. *Political and administrative jurisdictions* provides a means of relating the parcel to the jurisdictions that affect it. All parcels, for example, are typically in a county and at least one school district. Larger agencies, such as police, public works, and motor vehicle departments, often have geographic subdivisions for administrative purposes. The codes for the jurisdictions can be used both to identify the jurisdictions into which a particular parcel falls and to aggregate parcels by jurisdiction.

8. *Physical block* identification enables agencies that have a block numbering system to key any given city block to all parcels in that block.

9. *Lot position* notes any positional characteristics of the lot, such as whether it forms a corner or is in a key or reverse alignment with respect to adjoining lots.

10. *Maps on which the parcel is mapped* lists the public agency map

records which include the parcel. Many state and local governments map areas for such different purposes as zoning, drainage, assessment, structural regulation, or fire control. These maps provide a composite of information about the parcel, and the parcel record notation would provide an index to their existence and locations.

Land and Structural Characteristics

11. *Parcel size* gives the dimensions and area of the parcel. Since urban lots are generally rectangular, front width and average depth can be recorded in feet. Area can either be calculated by a computer from length-width data or the total area itself can be recorded. For large parcels or those of irregular size, the acreage can be indicated.

12. *Zoning* to indicate permitted land usage is identified for all parcels to which it applies. Various modifications of the zone, such as variances and exceptions affecting the parcel, can be shown where applicable.

13. *Master plan category and plans affecting parcel* shows future plans of government agencies that affect the parcel. For example, if it has been designated for acquisition as a flood-control-settling basin, school site, or highway route, this fact can be recorded as soon as the decision is made by the agency involved. Other types of plans, such as a conservation priority rating, can also be noted.

14. *Land use(s)* indicates the use of the parcel, such as for growing grapes, manufacturing automobiles, or housing people. The use category should be coded to a level of detail that will satisfy all users of this information. For example, a city planner might be satisfied to know that rural land is used for agricultural purposes, but the agricultural commissioner would need to know what kind of grain is grown on the land. Where "activity on premises" differs from basic land use, such additional data could be included. Each separate use on the same parcel could be separately identified with the area of the parcel devoted to that use. Information describing the occupant, such as Standard Industrial Classification Code, would be included under Owner-Occupant characteristics (see item 52a.).

15. *Assessed value* is the current assessed value of the land, improvements, trees, vines, and personal property, each separately shown.

16. *Exemptions* records the exemptions to which the owner of the parcel is entitled, such as those for veterans and homeowners.

17. *Taxable value* is the value of the parcel on which taxes are computed.

18. *Tax delinquency* identifies any unpaid taxes on the parcel and the number of years that payment is delinquent. Technical sale of the property to the state for nonpayment of taxes can be noted.

19. *Liens, assessments, and encumbrances* records either complete de-

scriptive information, such as the specific amount and creditor of a sewer assessment, mortgage, or mechanic's lien, or simply a reference code to the existence of such data about the parcel in another specified file. Bonded debt affecting the parcel and "benefit footage" of any assessments could also be included.

20. *Deed restrictions* includes the type and effective date of restrictions.

21. *Easements* records the type, holder, and location of easements on the parcel.

22. *Water and/or mineral rights* appurtenant to the parcel includes the holder(s) of such rights.

23. *Topographic characteristics* includes elevation, degree and direction of slope, unusual earthquake sensitivity, whether the parcel includes cut or fill land, land bearing capacity, and subsidence.

24. *Drainage characteristics* records whether the parcel is subject to flooding or erosion problems, and such characteristics as rainfall recorded by a measuring station located on the parcel. Water table level below the parcel can also be shown.

25. *Soil type* includes such information about the soil as permeability, mineral composition, root zone, and rockiness.

26. *Productivity data* lists the agricultural or timber production of the parcel, such as type of crop and amount of yield.

27. *Extractive data* describes minerals and oils existing in or extracted from the parcel.

28. *Fish and wildlife data* includes types and numbers of animals in various agency programs. Agricultural pests can also be noted.

29. *Date of last sale of parcel* indicates the date when the parcel was last sold.

30. *Price at last sale of parcel* shows either the actual amount when known, or as indicated by tax stamps on the deed.

31. *Rental price* is the amount of rental payments if the parcel is rented or leased.

32. *Building characteristics.* Into this subcategory fall all the data that describe the structures on a parcel:

a. *Number of separate buildings.*
b. *Floor area of building(s).*
c. *Portion of parcel covered by building(s).*
d. *Setback of building(s)*—side, front, and rear.
e. *Frontage and depth of building(s).*
f. *Height of building(s).*
g. *Number of stories in building(s).*
h. *Number of rooms in building(s).*
i. *Existence of basement(s).*
j. *Number of dwelling units in building(s).*

k. *Type and class of building construction.*
l. *Cost of building construction.*
m. *Year building(s) built.*
n. *Condition of building(s).* This would code objective and subjective data describing the physical condition of the structure.
o. *Number and character of all licenses and permits pertaining to the structures* (boiler, gas pump, elevator, oil well, storage tanks, etc.).

33. *Utilities connected* shows the connection of gas, water, and electric meters and telephones to the building(s) and the size of the meters. Data that concern the consumption of these commodities could also be accumulated.

34. *Waste disposal facilities* describes sewage facilities, special industrial output such as chemical wastes, sanitary facilities, and the presence of such facilities as garbage disposals.

35. *Presence of civil defense facility,* such as a shelter or first aid station, could be identified and its capacity and stockpiled supplies recorded.

36. *Presence of special establishments,* for example, those that emit air pollutants or use radioactive substances or devices such as X rays can be identified.

37. *Presence of swimming pool* indicates whether a swimming pool is on the parcel.

38. *Police information* relates events requiring police attention to the parcels where they occurred. Information items can include, for crimes and incidents, the type, date, time, and case number.

39. *Fire information* includes information of primary concern in fire prevention and suppression, such as the following:

a. *Fires at this parcel*—kind, date, loss.
b. *Fire alarm responses to this parcel*—date, type (for example, false).
c. *Fire prevention inspection record.*
  (1.) *Date of last inspection.*
  (2.) *Violations noted.*
  (3.) *Special hazards identified*—flammable liquids, acids, explosives, incinerator.
d. *Rooms certified for maximum occupants.*
e. *Presence of automatic fire sprinklers, standpipes, extinguishers.*
f. *Presence of fire walls.*
g. *Rescue/ambulance responses to this parcel.*
h. *Distance from parcel to nearest fire hydrant and fire alarm box.*

40. *Public health information* includes data of primary concern in public health functions, such as the following:

a. *Health hazard conditions at this parcel.*
b. *Diseases reported at this parcel.*

c. *Health permits* (for example, if it is a food-vending establishment).

d. *Inspection record*—see 39c. for details.

41. *Automobiles registered at this parcel* lists license numbers of automobiles registered at the parcel.

42. *Subsurface structures and improvements* identifies the presence and ownership of structures below the surface of the parcel, such as mineshafts, sewers, tanks, or storm drains.

43. *Neighborhood characteristics* describes general environmental conditions in the area of the parcel. The area might be defined as a voting precinct, census block, tract, or a department administrative district such as a water-meter-reading route. Characteristics can be defined in subjective, judgmental terms such as "developing," "stationary," "declining," or "blighted." They can also be related to such features as noise, vibration, local smoke, and glare. Other characteristics, such as library, recreational, or social welfare needs, can also be identified.

44. *Proximity to special facilities* identifies the distance of the parcel from such facilities as schools, parks, railroads, rivers, and freeways. Distance could be recorded either "as the crow flies," by walking, or street route.

45. *Personal property at parcel* identifies all items of personal property about which specific information exists, such as guns, dogs, and boats. Property registration numbers should be listed for items that have been assigned such numbers.

Owner-Occupant Characteristics

46. *Owner's name and mailing address* can include any special ownership conditions, such as probate or trusteeship status, as well as direct ownership.

47. *Occupants' name(s)* includes persons, "doing business as" designations, and common terms by which structures are referred to, as, for example, the "Rose Bowl."

48. *Occupancy group* describes the basic category into which the occupant falls, as defined by such classifications as the Uniform Building Code. Classifications in this Code measure the hazard to persons or property caused by the type of building occupancy. For example, the least hazard exists in accessory buildings and the greatest in assembly halls with stages and capacity to hold more than 1000 persons.

49. *Vacancy information as applicable* notes if the structure on the parcel is vacant.

50. *Number and kind of licenses and permits granted to occupants* can identify important characteristics of real property if *all* licenses and permits issued by all agencies are related to the parcel occupied by the

licensee. Such licensees include doctors, barbers, businesses of any kind, and automobile drivers.

51. *Residential occupant characteristics* include data about persons using the parcel as their domicile. Some of the data may not be available on a parcel-by-parcel basis, but averages for the census tract or block in which the parcel is located can be recorded.

  a. *Number of occupants.*
  b. *Number of households.*
  c. *Number of occupants per room.*
  d. *Race of occupants.*
  e. *Sex of occupants.*
  f. *Age of occupants*—month and year born.
  g. *Education of occupants*—years of school completed.
  h. *Family income class.*
  i. *Voters' registration of occupants.*
  j. *Occupation(s) of occupants* described in such terms as those in the *Dictionary of Occupational Titles.*
  k. *Major industrial groups* in which occupants are employed.
  l. *Employment status* includes such data as the full- or part-time status of workers, unemployment status, and period of time out of work.
  m. *Place of work* identifies by parcel number, grid coordinate, or other location index where the occupants work.
  n. *Means of transportation to work* reveals whether private automobile, walking, or public vehicle is normally used by these occupants.
  o. *Tenure of household head* shows when the present occupants began their occupancy; prior address could also be shown.
  p. *Occupants rent or own?*
  q. *Occupants receiving public welfare services or assistance* lists this fact and the type of service or category of aid received.
  r. *Occupants with criminal or correction records* includes such categories as released convicts, parolees, and juveniles and adults on probation.
  s. *Children in school* includes data for both public and private institutions and the numbers and grades of the children involved. Preschool children would be revealed by age data (see 51f.).
  t. *Birth-death data* relates these events to this parcel.

52. *Commercial/industrial occupant characteristics.*

  a. *Type of business(es)* at the parcel can be identified by Standard Industrial Classification Code, business license groups, or other categorizations that will supplement the land-use information item (item 14) for commercial and industrial occupants.
  b. *Parcel number(s) of other parcels comprising store or plant site* permits all adjacent parcels used by this occupant to be identified.
  c. *Number of employees* is shown for each occupying business, separately listed if several businesses occupy the parcel.

d. *Employee place of residence* summarizes by category, such as census tract or grid coordinate, the places of residence of the persons working at this parcel.

e. *Means of transportation used in getting to work* refers to classes of employees using automobile, public transportation, etc.

f. *Off-street parking spaces provided* by the business.

g. *Labor force data* includes such aggregate information about the employees as salary class, sex, employee accidents, or occupational type.

h. *Retail sales* contains data giving the dollar value of taxable goods sold in any given time period.

i. *Business failures* at parcel can be recorded.

Street Section Record Item Definitions

The street section is a defined portion of right of way. Such right of way may be an alley, as well as a street. All the recorded characteristics of a particular street section form the street section record.

1. *Section number* is the numerical reference to the street section.

2. *Section name* is the official name of the street section.

3. *Section class* identifies the street section as being local, collector, arterial, freeway, alley, etc.

4. *Section status* codes the street as being public or private.

5. *Section direction*—north, south, etc.

6. *Section limits* lists the termini of the section, by intersecting section numbers, political jurisdiction boundaries, etc.

7. *Section length* can be identified in miles or mile fractions.

8. *Intersecting sections* gives the street sections that cross the section here referenced.

9. *Intersection code* is the reference number of the intersection(s) itself.

10. *Jurisdiction code(s)* identifies the political and administrative jurisdictions into which the section falls.

11. *Section width* identifies the section width measured to the limits of the right of way.

12. *Street width* identifies the width of the street paving (curb to curb).

13. *Section surface type* lists the surface material of the street; for example, 4-inch concrete on 8-inch aggregate rock base, or oil on gravel.

14. *Section surface condition* indicates the condition of the surface according to classification by inspectors.

15. *Grade* identifies the slope(s) in the section.

16. *Alignment* describes any curvature in the section.

17. *Drainage conditions* indicates any flooding or drainage problems associated with the section.

18. *Traffic volume data* lists such items as current, projected, and capacity vehicle volume figures for the section.

19. *Parking space data* shows the number of spaces and whether they are marked on the street.

20. *Presence of parking meters* along section lists the number of parking meters and can include the revenue derived from each.

21. *Presence of curbs*—height, year built, condition, etc.

22. *Presence of sidewalks*—width, year built, condition, etc.

23. *Presence of street lights*—wattage, year installed, pole number, etc.

24. *Presence of sewers*—precise location, map reference, capacity, condition, etc.

25. *Presence of storm drains*—precise location, capacity, condition, map reference, etc.

26. *Presence of street trees*—kind, year planted, date pruned and sprayed, etc.

27. *Presence of utility facilities* includes telephones and electrical, water, and gas lines, their precise location, map reference, etc.

28. *Presence of structures* identifies grade crossings, bridges, and tunnels along the section, and their condition and capacity.

29. *Presence of traffic signals, stop signs, and other traffic control devices*—type, timing, age.

30. *Public transportation facilities* and services along the section, including the location of bus benches.

31. *Traffic accident data* for section can include the day, time, and types of accidents and the case numbers.

32. *Street and curb markings* indicates whether the section is striped for lane control, has "no parking" designations, or posted markings such as "school ahead."

33. *Speed limits* for section.

34. *Fire alarm boxes* along section.

35. *Plans affecting section* includes data describing projected street widenings, surface improvements, subsurface facility installations, etc.

36. *Deficiencies* in structures and facilities can be noted.

37. *Parcel numbers of adjacent parcels* lying along the section can be listed.

Person Record Item Definitions

I. *Identity Data*

1. *Name.* In addition to last, first, and middle names, the following items should be included when applicable: "also known as," aliases, maiden name, former names, "doing business as" designations, and similar categories which identify a person by name. Soundex code designations when used would constitute a separate file which could serve as an index to the System file.

2. *Social Security number.* Social Security number, as the currently and potentially most comprehensive number system relating to persons, can be the basic numerical identifier.

3. *Sex.*

4. *Date of birth* and birth certificate number as filed in the appropriate governmental office.

5. *Place of birth,* including city, county, state, and country, if necessary.

6. *Date of death* and certificate number is a useful item since inquiries are often made about persons whose demise is unknown to the inquirer.

7. *Place of death,* including city, county, state, and country, if necessary.

8. *Race/descent.*

9. *Religion* is an item of little interest to most functions, but is recorded by others as part of the basic information describing a particular individual. Since it is collected by very few functions, it would not be an item filed for most of the persons described in the System.

10. *Current address,* showing the street address where the person maintains his domicile, together with

    a. *Date moved to current address.*

    b. *Permanent address,* if current address is temporary.

11. *Previous address(es)* for, say, the past ten years.

12. *Date came to state,* if not evident from above.

13. *Date came to county,* if not evident from above.

14. *Height.*

15. *Weight.*

16. *Color of eyes.*

17. *Color of hair.*

18. *Complexion of skin.*

19. *Marks and scars.*

20. *Physical handicaps* specifying any handicaps that clearly relate to the identification of an individual, such as blindness, amputations, and continuous wearing of glasses.

21. *Blood type.*

22. *Marital status* indicates whether the person is married, single, divorced, widowed, or separated.

    a. *Date and place of marriage(s).*

    b. *Name of spouse,* and spouse's Social Security number.

    c. *Names of former spouses* and Social Security numbers.

    d. *Data describing any divorce decrees,* such as court, decree number, and date.

23. *Citizenship,* listing the country of which the person is a citizen.

    a. *Alien status number* is given if the person is an alien.

    b. *Naturalization number* is shown for naturalized citizens.

24. *Fingerprint classification* lists the code numbers for the classification of the person's fingerprints. These classification code numbers are a

series of digits based on the loops and whorls of the fingers. Classifications are assigned by local law enforcement agencies, state criminal identification bureaus, and the Federal Bureau of Investigation.

25. *Military service.* Specific items describing military service should include:

a. *Period of service.*
b. *Branch of service.*
c. *Type of discharge.*
d. *Service serial number.*

26. *Selective Service number* is the number assigned to persons registered by the Selective Service System.

27. *Parents' names and Social Security numbers* refers to the parents of the individual. Mother's maiden name can also be recorded here.

28. *Children's names and Social Security numbers* refers to the children of the individual and their relationship, whether normal, adopted, foster, etc.

29. *Siblings' names and Social Security numbers* refers to brothers and sisters. Detailed data about parents, children, or siblings are available in the records for the persons referenced.

II. *Status Data*

A. *Voters' Registration Status* identifies whether the person is or has been registered and includes:

30. *Party affiliation.*
31. *Precinct.*
32. *Elections in which vote cast,* used to purge voters' register.

B. *Licenses and Permits* are probably the major regulatory instrument used by state and local governments, as they authorize actions which are otherwise illegal. Licenses and permits fall into four basic categories: *business, construction, operating,* and *professional and vocational.* In each case, the form of information on the license itself is essentially the same and would be maintained for each license and permit as follows:

33. *Type of license or permit.*
34. *Number.*
35. *Date issued.*
36. *Expiration date* (if any).
37. *Issuing agency.*
38. *Special conditions,* which include any special requirements, such as wearing glasses to operate an automobile.

C. *Law Enforcement Data.* Law enforcement agencies generally assign identification numbers to persons with whom they have had any contact. Such persons are victims, suspects, informants, or offenders of record.

Numbers are issued by local sheriff and police departments, by state bureaus of criminal identification and investigation, by the FBI, and by special law enforcement agencies, such as state narcotics bureaus and district attorneys' offices. It is important that all numbers be listed, since the completeness of listing provides a useful means of ensuring the correct identity of the person involved. These numbers are shown as items 39b., 40e., and 41b., below. Law enforcement data themselves consist primarily of the following categories:

39. *Outstanding warrants* that have been issued for the arrest of a person and have not yet been served upon him. The serving of such warrants is the obligation of any law enforcement agency if it can locate the person named. The following warrant information items are useful to all such agencies:

    a. *Issuing court.*
    b. *Law enforcement agency involved* and identifying number assigned by the agency.
    c. *Offense charged.*
    d. *Date of warrant.*
    e. *Warrant number.*

40. *Offense record* describes the specific incidents and offenses in which the person has been involved either as a victim, suspect, informant, or charged offender. Items of information within this group are as follows:

    a. *Type of offense(s)* indicates the code section violated or the kind of offense involved. Traffic violations can be included here and would be useful where auto insurance rates or driver's license terms are based on traffic violation history.
    b. *Date of offense(s).*
    c. *Case or record number(s)* gives the number assigned by the appropriate law enforcement agency to each offense involving this person. Many persons, of course, have been involved in numerous offenses and incidents, so this particular item of data could be quite extensive.
    d. *Disposition* indicates what has been done about each offense. It tells, for example, whether the case is closed for lack of evidence or suspects, or has been disposed of through the judicial process, or has been referred to other designated law enforcement agencies.
    e. *Law enforcement agency or agencies* lists those agencies that have been concerned with offenses and incidents involving this person.

41. *Ex-convict registration number* refers to the number assigned to a person who has completed a sentence after having been convicted of an offense. Registration is often a requirement both at the time a person is released from prison and at the time he takes up residence in a local community. Necessary items of data in this category are as follows:

a. *Registration date.*

b. *Law enforcement agency involved* and the identifying number assigned by the agency.

42. *Missing persons data* include:

a. *Date reported missing.*

b. *Location last known.*

c. *Law enforcement agency involved.*

D. *Court Actions* in which the person has been involved includes:

43. *Plaintiff and defendant,* indicating role of person concerned.

44. *Court.*

45. *Case number.*

46. *Type of action,* for example, civil or probate.

47. *Date.*

48. *Disposition.*

E. *Probation/Parole Data* generally describes persons who are not in custody but with whose behavior and whereabouts a law enforcement agency has special concern. In the case of probation, the person is either an adult or a juvenile who has been granted authorization by the court to remain a member of free society but with special conditions and supervision by the probation officer. Parolees have served a period of time in prison and are completing their sentence outside the prison walls, under the supervision of a parole officer. Data items relating to probation and parole are as follows:

49. *Probation or parole number,* as assigned by the appropriate agency.

50. *Court and case number,* as assigned by the appropriate court.

51. *Probation or parole agency.*

52. *Offense* (or delinquent act in the case of juveniles).

53. *Date* that person began his status as a probationer or parolee.

54. *Term of probation or parole.*

55. *Special conditions,* such as frequency of required reporting to parole or probation officer and limitations on freedom of movements.

F. *Employment Data* includes:

56. *Current employer.*

57. *Employer number,* as assigned by the appropriate agency.

58. *Employer address.*

59. *Date employed.*

60. *Employer Standard Industrial Classification Code.*

61. *Previous employers,* with addresses, dates employed, and employers' numbers.

62. *Occupation of person,* that is, his vocation or specialization, such as whether he is an accountant, a physician, a physicist, a cosmetologist, or a data systems analyst.

63. *Unemployment date,* the date at which a person became currently unemployed.

64. *Earnings within the past year* would list the reportable wages received by the person as required by unemployment and disability compensation programs.

65. *Payments received* from unemployment and disability compensation programs. Specific amounts paid to the person in benefits.

G. *Confinement Data* relates to persons either currently or previously confined in institutions under public auspices, such as hospitals, prisons, and charity homes.

66. *Type of confinement* specifies whether the person was confined for penal violations, mental deficiency, physical disease, etc.

67. *Period of confinement.*

68. *Place of confinement* lists public institution or private facility.

69. *Reason for confinement* includes the actions leading to confinement, such as the offense or the particular mental or physical condition responsible for the person's being institutionalized.

70. *Commitment authorization* specifies the legal authority by which the person is detained (if applicable) and the person or agency responsible for the detention.

71. *Treatment data* describes the kind of treatment given to the person within the institution(s) where he has been confined, and notations on its effects.

72. *Confinement escapes* relates to the where, when, and how of any escapes from confinement made by this person.

H. *Welfare Data* describes the circumstances relating to the receipt of any kind of public assistance. Specific data items include:

73. *County case number.*

74. *State case number.*

75. *Category of aid received.*

76. *Amount of aid received.*

77. *Periods during which aid received,* both current and past.

78. *Basis for aid* gives specifics as to the circumstances under which aid was required and authorized.

I. *Health Data* describes any data about the person's health that are of public concern and record.

79. *Physical deficiencies* includes any handicaps not described in the identity data section.

80. *Reportable diseases,* such as diabetes and tuberculosis, affecting the person would be noted as well as the date of onset, treatment data, and indication of effectiveness of treatments undertaken.

81. *Special conditions* includes any special circumstances related to health, such as a requirement that the person report to his local health

officer on specified dates because of the communicability of diseases with which he has been afflicted.

82. *Immunization and X-ray data* can be kept to indicate X rays and/or immunization and the date and location where given.

J. *Educational Data* lists the formal schooling and such related information about the person as the following:

83. *Schools attended* by name and location.

84. *Periods of attendance* at each school.

85. *Courses completed,* including any major subjects studied or special curricula completed.

86. *Degrees granted.*

87. *Intelligence or achievement test results* that are available.

K. *Miscellaneous Data* includes such items as the following:

88. *Income tax bureau number.*

a. *Year(s) return filed.*
b. *Income tax group* or specific amount reported by the person.
c. *Number and name(s) of dependents claimed.*

89. *Parcel numbers of real property* owned would provide a cross index to the real property file.

90. *Registration numbers of personal property,* such as automobiles, guns, scales, boats, and airplanes, serves as a cross reference to the personal property owned by this individual.

91. *Registration numbers of firms in which a person is involved* as partner, owner, etc., provides cross index to appropriate files.

92. *Organization memberships,* such as unions, lodges, juvenile gangs, can be noted where the information is of public record.

93. *Government agencies* not identified from the reference codes in the various groups of status data above can be specified where they have additional information on this person, and the kind of information they possess can be noted. For example, if the Department of Agriculture has specific information on a few persons, the fact that such information exists in that department can be noted in the record of those persons and an indication given concerning the character of the information.

PRINCIPLES OF DATA SYSTEM DESIGN

This appendix presents some principles to guide agencies in the development of data systems. These principles supplement the discussion of steps toward implementation of the Unified Information System and relate to designing the complete information system of a particular agency. Such agency information systems handle all the environmental and internal data with which an agency is concerned.

Many of the principles are similar for all organizations; a few are peculiar to state and local government agencies. It is not our purpose to present a check list covering every step to be taken in designing a data system; a number of excellent volumes already provide this information.[1] Our purpose, in keeping with the conceptual character of this study, is to identify the major principles that state and local governments should observe in data system design.

Data system design specifies in comprehensive terms the role played by information in an organization. Designing a data system involves more than the frequently discussed "feasibility study" that usually determines whether or not a particular piece or class of data processing equipment is practicable. Such a determination should be a terminal step in data system design. Understanding and properly specifying the role of information involve the following general principles of data system design:

1. *Emphasis on the objectives of the organization.* In an important sense, information is the commodity that holds any organization together. Without information describing its operations and environment, an organization would cease to function. Data relate the organization to its environment and the components of the organization to each other. It is therefore essential that the data system be designed to further the organization's objectives. Although this may appear to be a manifest truism, many or-

---

[1] See Appendix E.

ganizations are served by data systems that have grown up in the hodge-podge manner of historical convenience, which precludes them from efficiently serving the organization's current objectives. Therefore, at the beginning of the data system design endeavor, it is useful to take a fresh look at objectives and to write them in explicit form.

2. *Comprehensiveness.* For the purpose of initial analysis, the more comprehensive the viewpoint from which the design of a data system is undertaken, the better. This does not mean that only big systems are good systems. Rather, it means system design should *begin* at the most comprehensive level and then be scaled down as subsequent investigation indicates is appropriate. Since any data system, large or small, should further the organization's objectives, its design should recognize that data pervade an entire organization; they are seldom limited to a single department. A system, therefore, cannot be developed efficiently piece by isolated piece. The comprehensive approach is more promising and suggests several specific techniques:

(a) The persons conducting a data system design study should be located organizationally close to the top of the administrative structure, not confined to any one functional organization. Most administrative analysis activities in state and local governments are attached to top management, an arrangement that should certainly be followed in relation to data system designers. These designers will, of course, be supplemented by functional specialists when they are designing a system that includes data of particular use within one function. In general, however, a comprehensive viewpoint can be supplied only by a person whose loyalty is to an organization's central administrative group.

(b) Data system design is a continuing activity. It is not something that is completed once and for all; it specifically demands the establishment of permanent responsibility for data system analysis. Many state and local government agencies now recognize this demand and have assigned responsibility to a specific person or group. Almost universally such persons report difficulty in recruiting qualified personnel to conduct the analyses. Without offering any solution to this problem, we simply stress that as government increases in complexity and size, as we have earlier suggested it will, efficient information systems will become increasingly important. These must be designed by qualified people if they are going to work effectively. Government agencies should, therefore, place high priority on the recruitment, training, and retention of qualified data system analysis personnel.

(c) State and local governments must be equally as willing to spend dollars on data system design as they are on data processing equipment. Over the next several years, it is likely that the expense ratio will change to such an extent that the preponderance will shift to system design rather than to the equipment configuration required to implement the system.

3. *Focus attention on specific items of data.* It is well to remember that information systems from the smallest to the grandest are composed of individual, specific items of data. Data system design should focus on these items. The analysis sequence should be as follows: The first question to be asked is, "What data items are used in a particular task that is necessary to further the objectives earlier identified?" This deceptively simple sequence has not been followed in many data system studies. Too often, traditional procedures handed down over a period of years have merely been mechanized on some piece of data processing equipment. In such cases, there has been little or no analysis of the appropriateness of these procedures to the organization's objectives or of the *use* of the data these procedures require. This primary principle is simply to identify the purpose and use of data items needed for a particular task.

Once this question has been answered, and it may take many months for even a small organization, the system designer turns to the possible sources of data items that will provide the necessary inputs. Many items of input data are used as outputs without any change in their format. In other cases, there is a transformation of inputs into different outputs by such processes as aggregation, correlation, or computation.

It is important in this analysis of inputs and outputs that attention not be limited to what have traditionally been called "applications," such as accounting, payroll, and voters' registration. These applications usually have a strong orientation toward existing procedures. Focusing only on these applications defeats both the earlier principle of concentrating on organizational objectives and the principle stressed here of concentrating on the data items that serve these objectives.

4. *Specify the role of information in management decisions as well as clerical operations.* Since information is a major ingredient in all decision processes, data systems should provide the information that managers require. This means that the entire range of management decisions in an agency must be reviewed and the relevant data items identified; then, the more difficult task should be undertaken of specifying *how* these data are used in the decision process. Criteria, priorities, and other decision rules should be made as explicit as possible. Where a high degree of explicitness is achieved, consideration should be given to automating the decision process itself as well as the flow and storage of data. Using the full power of the computer for explicit decision-making can relieve human decision-makers of tedious tasks and enable them, in accordance with the management-by-exception principle, to devote themselves to more complex decisions that require extensive judgment.

5. *Analyze characteristics and movement of data.* Data items describe objects and events of concern to the organization for which the data system is designed. Many different data items are arranged into records with re-

spect to the object or event they describe. These data and records are sometimes used in the form in which they are filed. In other cases, they are aggregated into various kinds of reports. Broadly defined, a report could include an end product, such as a payroll check or a license, or some periodic aggregation of data for purposes of management planning or control. Between the collection of information in the form of input and its use as output reports, *transactions* occur to assemble the data, change them in some way, and prepare them for use. Data system analysis is concerned with these transactions by (1) type, (2) volume, and (3) time requirements.

In analyzing the movement of data, the traditional technique of flow charting is essential. Flow charts show the generation of data items and their movement within the organization through various transactions and into various reports. They also show the operations performed on the data and the tasks for which they are used. Another useful technique shows in tabular form the logical sequence of actions performed on the data. Again, we emphasize the importance of focusing on the data items rather than the forms used to convey them.

Based on the analysis of records, reports, and transactions, the system designer can begin to consider what equipment may be suitable for the system he is designing. It is important that equipment be matched to the characteristics of the job to be done at each phase: input, communications, processing, storage, and output. All the way from source-data automation on the input side to display and printing systems on the output side, equipment should be matched to the job—not vice versa. In the entire analysis, emphasis should be placed on where within an organization data originate and where they could originate; where data are used and where they could be used.

6. *Evaluate savings over a long period and more completely than by the sole criterion of personnel displaced.* There is a temptation to take only a short-range view of data systems, a direct comparison between the cost of the data processing equipment and the savings it will yield immediately. Far more significant in many cases are the long-term values to be gained through improved information system design. These benefits accrue from better decisions that better information can make possible. Such savings often accrue over a period of several years rather than at once, and they can be more significant to the objectives of the organization than the mere displacement of employees.

7. *Overcome fixation on hard copy records.* As electronic data processing equipment is more widely introduced into government agencies, the advantages of discontinuing paper records with visible characters written on them for persons to review will become increasingly apparent. The ultimate use of data must govern the question of records, not the form in which the data are stored. Government officials must orient themselves toward

the format for use rather than the medium of storage. There is no reason why data cannot be stored by electronic means, although they cannot in this form be physically handled like the traditional ledger card. Economies in electronic equipment for both storing and processing data will increase rapidly over the next few years. To maintain parallel records, one visible and one electronic, is both uneconomical and unnecessary. Here, as in many other places in data system design, concentration cannot properly be on *paper work* but should be on *data work*. The paper medium is relatively unimportant; it is simply a historical convenience that will become less acceptable as better media, especially electronics, are further developed.

8. *Integrate the collection of internal and environmental data where possible.* Although internal and environmental data would usually be stored in different files, they often could be gathered in the same transaction.

9. *Utilize existing data processing equipment.* Most state and local governments can profitably employ existing data processing equipment. Such equipment—either traditional punch card machinery controlled by plug boards or electronic devices controlled by internal programming—can be made available to agencies by several methods: (a) lease or purchase; (b) commercial service bureaus; (c) joint agency procurement and operation; and (d) rental of time on privately owned or leased machines. Many books and articles have dealt with equipment and the choice of methods for securing its use; such questions should be of terminal concern in data system design.[2] The system should be designed first, and appropriate equipment then procured to facilitate it. Most agencies can afford to invest two or three years in careful design of a data system. Too early fixation on hardware characteristics can quickly preclude objectivity. After the system has been designed, equipment and service bureau vendors can be asked to make proposals for implementing the system. These proposals should be evaluated in terms of the objectives and economics of the governmental unit. No universal rules apply to equipment selection except that the equipment should permit the data system to perform its specified functions. Normally, there is no reason to pay for equipment to provide more than this capability, although capacity for adding equipment modules as the system grows can be an important consideration.

A particular hazard to be avoided is that of succumbing to the dazzling allurements of various equipment components, regardless of their appropriateness to the system. Very fast printer speed, for example, may be totally irrelevant for a particular system. There is a special danger of becoming excessively impressed with speed for its own sake. The rule of fitting the appropriate equipment to the system is essential.

Particular attention should be given to devices permitting automatic or

---

[2] See also Appendix C.

semiautomatic input of data. Although reliable optical scanning of hand-recorded data is a few years away, several current devices can substantially reduce input problems. Marking spaces on punch cards with electrographic pencils and hand-portable card punching devices, and expanded use of raised letter templates for fixed data, are attractive ways to reduce clerical work in data collection. Punch cards are entirely suitable for storing data in small systems and provide simple, manual, random access, especially when they are interpreted, that is, when data recorded by holes are also printed on the face of the card. Processing equipment abounds. Communications within a small system can consist of telephonic inquiries to initiate manual retrieval from the central files and updating by physical movement of documents and/or punch cards prepared in decentralized locations. Existing data transmission hardware also can transmit digital data between remote points and a central processing and storage facility.

The Unified Information System concept of remote input and output, balanced with centralized storage and processing, can be applied directly to a system limited to a single government agency. The departments or their sections collect data and use them; the agency's information center stores and processes data according to department instructions.

Small governmental units may find it more economical to use the facilities of a service bureau or rent time on a privately owned or leased machine than to acquire their own complete set of equipment. Alternatively, several small agencies might set up a data processing center for their combined use, pooling the equipment. Several different arrangements are possible. The main point is that the final configuration, placement, and ownership of the equipment are secondary to the system it serves. The fact that small governmental agencies cannot afford their own computer installations does not mean they cannot design improved information systems in accordance with the principles outlined in this study.

EQUIPMENT EVALUATION AND SELECTION

This appendix presents a number of major points found valuable in preparing invitations to data processing equipment manufacturers to submit solutions to problems, and in evaluating their proposals.

No set of rules will apply to the analysis of all proposals for every application and organization; such analyses are necessarily individual. Certain general points, however, apply to all equipment selection. Here these points are discussed in the context of an organization contemplating acquiring its own equipment facility. The same points are relevant also to an agency considering any of the four methods by which equipment can be made available (noted in Appendix B).

In this discussion, it is assumed that the agency has designed a data system and now wishes to solicit equipment proposals. The system may ultimately be modified after a particular equipment configuration is selected (to take advantage of individual equipment characteristics), but the system described in the proposals should be one that would work successfully if installed as stated. In this respect, it is much more than a "bench-mark problem" in that it represents the best attempt at specification of a complete system.

The discussion is divided into four parts: (1) the request for proposals; (2) analysis of bidders' proposals; (3) comparison of bidders' proposals; and (4) deciding on a particular proposal.

THE REQUEST FOR PROPOSALS

To obtain meaningful proposals from manufacturers, the points below must be considered in the request for proposals. Those under "Presentation of the Problem" are also directly relevant to proposals requested from service organizations.

Presentation of the Problem

The problem should be presented to prospective bidders as a system which, if implemented, would accomplish the desired results—rather than as a scaled-down bench-mark problem. The system study determines that certain inputs and outputs are necessary and that certain items must be kept in files. The system description should specify in detail these required inputs, outputs, and files. It should also state precisely how the outputs are obtained from the input and file items so that bidders can determine the amount of processing and computing involved. Usually, a series of simple flow charts can describe the relationship among inputs, files, and outputs.

In these charts, the system must be divided arbitrarily into equipment processing procedures or runs, *only* for the purpose of describing the problem and indicating a possible solution. The bidders must understand that they are free to rearrange the runs as they see fit, combining runs or dividing single runs into several different ones. The only restriction is that their solutions must produce the required outputs from the indicated inputs and file items. Since bidders' personnel usually have had considerable systems experience and are often able to contribute new ideas for solving the problems, requests for proposals should try to avoid rigid restrictions on the input and output formats, and especially on the file configuration.

In addition to flow charts, a brief narrative describing each application and what it accomplishes should be included. Such a description gives a useful over-all picture of the total problem area.

In describing each input, output, and file in the request for proposals, the following points should be included for each document and file:

Input Documents

(1) Purpose of the document: how it is originated and what it accomplishes in the processing.
(2) Description of each information item (field) on the document.
(3) Maximum length, average length, and percentage of use of each item.
(4) Maximum and average number of characters per document.
(5) Maximum and average number of such documents per time period.
(6) Any special information pertaining to the document.

Output Documents

(1) Purpose of the document.
(2) Description of each information item on the document.
(3) Maximum length, average length, and percentage of use of each information item.
(4) Maximum and average number of characters per document.
(5) Maximum and average number of records per document (when a document consists of many records, such as a tabulated listing).

(6) Maximum and average number of documents per time period.

(7) Exact format of the document, whenever no deviation can be accepted. If a specific format must be adhered to, the format must be shown. The exact size of the form, the number of lines of printing, and the number of blank lines must be shown. This information is important for the timing of printing operations.

(8) Time requirements.

(9) Any special information pertaining to the document, such as time deadlines.

Files

(1) Description of each information item in the file.

(2) Maximum and average length of each information item in the file.

(3) Maximum and average number of records per file.

Scope of Solution. Bidders must be cautioned to solve the problem given, so that in comparing proposals any differences in equipment, timing, etc., will not be due to dissimilarities in the problems solved. After a particular bidder's equipment has been selected, the problem will no doubt be changed considerably before actual operations begin in order to take advantage of the unique features of the equipment configuration selected. However, these changes should not be seriously considered until the proposals have been compared for the solution to the particular problem as originally specified.

Bidders should be told to inquire immediately if they have any doubts about the system in order to avoid submitting unacceptable solutions through misunderstanding. The bidder, not the customer, is responsible for the acceptability of a bid.

Utilization of Equipment

The request for proposals should state whether the problem areas shown in the bid are intended to use the equipment 100 per cent of the time, or whether a certain amount of free time is desired for possible future expansion of applications. If free time is desired, the amount must be specified. Depending on the type of equipment proposed, the desired amount of expansion can sometimes be provided with little idle time at the outset by adding various components as needed in a modular, or building-block, fashion. In any case, the manufacturer should be told what percentage of the total applications is represented in the request for proposals.

Checking

Although each bidder will generally indicate many checking devices and techniques in his solutions to the systems problem, any specific checks required by the agency should be indicated so that they can be incorporated in the bidder's solutions.

Timing Details

Bidders will give estimated times for each operation but will often omit details for this timing unless specifically requested. Although the details for all machine timing are not necessary, it is a good idea to request the manufacturer to indicate his bases for the timing of the operations and to give details for the major (most-used) loops of each machine program.

ANALYSIS OF BIDDERS' PROPOSALS

In studying the bidders' proposals, a careful analysis should be made of the several different aspects of each bid.

The Problem Solutions

The solutions submitted must be studied thoroughly to determine that they are reasonable, workable solutions that satisfy the requirements for inputs, outputs, and files.

Timing

The timing given in the proposal will have to be checked to determine that it is reasonably accurate. It should be emphasized that no solution can be timed accurately to the millisecond at this stage, since the number and types of program steps required in all cases will necessarily be estimates. Besides, these estimates are based on estimates—the problem itself as presented in the request for proposals. Consequently, the best that can be done is to analyze the timing and the bases for the timing to determine their reasonableness. An experienced analyst can perform these estimates. State and local governments should consider retaining consultants for verifying timing estimates for particular machines. It must be remembered that ascertaining the actual time required can be done only when a problem is programmed and run on a particular machine.

Checking

The proposed systems should indicate the checking devices that will be employed to ensure accuracy of processing. This is especially important when a new or different technique is being proposed and the method of control is not apparent. In most cases, however, if the method of checking is not shown, it is probably one that can be adapted to generally accepted techniques. Care must be taken to determine that all parts of the system are adequately controlled by either stated or implied methods.

Equipment and Price

Is the equipment adequate to do the work in the time specified? The answer, of course, is determined when the timing estimates are verified. Any serious timing errors can cause an adjustment in equipment complement and a resulting adjustment in price.

Automatic Programming

An effort should be made to determine the availability of automatic programming languages and what they will do. If such languages are being used, it is advisable to ask a user how successful they have proven. If the languages are not yet in use, a talk with the bidder's programming personnel may help in determining the details of the programs and when they will be debugged and ready for use.

Production Status

If the equipment recommended by a manufacturer has been in successful use, there is probably little question that it will arrive on the delivery date. However, if the equipment is new and untried, a visit to the manufacturer may be necessary to determine if the quoted delivery date is reasonable in view of the evident progress. In addition, if possible, it is advantageous to consult former customers to determine the manufacturer's past reliability in meeting quoted delivery dates.

Customer Service

Customer service is as important as the equipment itself. A good piece of equipment can be almost useless—especially to an inexperienced user— if the manufacturer does not give adequate service. This service must include the training of customer personnel to program the equipment and use it effectively, the issuance of up-to-date programming aids and manuals, and the assignment of manufacturer personnel to work closely with the customer in giving aid and advice in both systems analysis and programming. The question of customer service can best be answered by talking to present customers of the manufacturer to determine not only how satisfied they are with the service provided but that they are not overly biased for or against the manufacturer.

Emergency Machine

If the applications being considered have to be carried out within certain time limits (as do most state and local government applications), the availability of an emergency machine must be seriously considered. If the manufacturer has one in the area, there will probably be no problem in using it. However, if the use of a similar machine of another customer is planned, an agreement should be obtained before making a final decision on the equipment.

Other concerns are important to the user but, as a rule, they are not vital enough to influence his decision on whether to accept a proposal. The costs they represent are usually about the same for the various proposals. Only if two or more proposals are nearly equal in every other respect might such conditions as these become determining factors: (1) space and air-conditioning requirements, (2) installation costs, (3) manufacturer's definition of a shift and the method of charging for premium time and downtime, (4) free program-testing machine time.

COMPARISON OF BIDDERS' PROPOSALS

The following are points to be kept in mind in comparing proposals. This discussion assumes that proposals have been analyzed individually and that more than one proposal (as adjusted for equipment complement and price, if necessary) could do the work satisfactorily.

Individual Machine Characteristics

There is a tendency to judge proposals by comparing their individual hardware characteristics. This method of comparison is usually meaningless since, in the separate analyses of the proposals, all the characteristics of the machines were considered when it was determined if the problem solutions and times were reasonable. Once this is done, there is no reason to compare machines for size of memory, density of tape, speed of tape units, arithmetic speeds, printer speeds, etc. These characteristics are important, but only as they apply to the solution of the problem; taken by themselves they are unimportant. In fact, it seems that any equipment system has a particular application at which it is more efficient than other equipment systems— even though its characteristics may not sound impressive when considered alone.

Conversely, machine characteristics that a manufacturer regards as advantages may actually be disadvantages in certain applications. Very few "advantages" are universal. Some printers, for example, rated at a line-per-minute speed of up to four times that of other printers cannot print certain types of forms as fast as their slower counterparts. Such printers are faster only if their characteristics can be used to advantage in the applications concerned. In summary, the only true test is to compare complete hardware systems designed for a specific application or group of applications.

Possibility of Expansion

If it is expected that a great many applications will be added to the system in the next few years, the equipment's amenability to modular expansion is important. One should probably not plan modular expansion further ahead than five years, however, because the technology is changing so rapidly that in that time a completely new type of hardware is likely to be on the market.

The ability to remove units from the proposed equipment complement is also important. If the proposed complement includes idle time for possible expansion, then the ability to reduce the hardware system to the minimum size to accomplish the immediate work and subsequently to add to it as the expansion of applications requires can mean a large saving during the period of the initial system installation.

Comparative Costs

In comparing proposals, care must be taken to ensure that they are intended to accomplish the same work in computations, inputs, outputs, keypunching, verifying, etc. If they are not, the bids should be adjusted in respect to equipment (and price) so that they are comparable.

Probability of Fulfilling Commitments

Some estimate will have to be made of the relative probabilities that the manufacturers will meet their promised commitments of hardware delivery and customer service. The ability to meet delivery deadlines can be gauged to a great extent by determining the relative status of production of the various equipments and the number of such installations that will precede the one proposed. These relative probabilities can usually be determined only by consulting with the manufacturers' previous customers and with the manufacturers themselves.

Deciding on a Particular Proposal

One or more proposals can usually be eliminated at once as being entirely out of line with the others. The remaining proposals will have many features, such as air conditioning and space that are essentially the same for all and consequently can be ignored.

As for the remaining features, it must be a policy decision for the user to decide which ones are the most important to him. If cost overrides all else, he will select the cheapest system regardless of other features (since it has been established that any of them will do the job). However, other factors, such as promised delivery date, expected service, reports of users of similar equipment, availability of an emergency machine, or individual equipment characteristics may be more important than cost. In short, there is no absolute and universal criterion. The true purpose of the evaluation is to make all the factors and alternatives known to those persons responsible for making the final decision so that they accurately understand the alternatives and are actually making the decision they think they are making.

MAJOR DATA PROCESSING EQUIPMENT
MANUFACTURERS

The following is a list of some major data processing equipment manu-facturers, with the addresses of their national offices.

Burroughs Corporation
  6071 Second Avenue
  Detroit 32, Michigan

Control Data Corporation
  Computer Division
  501 Park Avenue
  Minneapolis 15, Minnesota

General Electric Company
  Computer Department
  13430 North Black Canyon Highway
  Phoenix, Arizona

International Business Machines Corporation
  590 Madison Avenue
  New York 22, New York

Minneapolis-Honeywell Regulator Company
  Electronic Data Processing Division
  60 Walnut Street
  Wellesley Hills 81, Massachusetts

Monroe Calculating Machine Company, Inc.
  555 Mitchell Street
  Orange, New Jersey

National Cash Register Company
  Main at K Streets
  Dayton 9, Ohio

Packard Bell Company
  1905 Armacost Avenue
  Los Angeles 25, California

Philco Corporation
    3000 Welsh Road
    Willow Grove, Pennsylvania
Radio Corporation of America
    Electronic Data Processing Division
    Front and Cooper Streets
    Camden, New Jersey
Royal McBee Corporation
    Data Processing Division
    Port Chester, New York
Univac Division
    Sperry Rand Corporation
    315 Park Avenue South
    New York 10, New York

BIBLIOGRAPHY

PERIODICALS AND DATA PROCESSING INFORMATION SERVICES

1. *Automatic Data Processing Service Newsletter* (bi-weekly)
   John Diebold & Associates, Inc.
   430 Park Avenue
   New York 22, New York
2. *Business Automation* (monthly)
   288 Park Avenue West
   Elmhurst, Illinois
3. *Computers & Automation* (monthly)
   815 Washington Street
   Newtonville 60, Massachusetts
4. *Data Processing* (monthly)
   22nd Floor, Book Tower
   Detroit 26, Michigan
5. *Data Processing Digest* (monthly)
   1140 South Robertson Boulevard
   Los Angeles 35, California
6. *Datamation* (monthly)
   10373 West Pico Boulevard
   Los Angeles 64, California
7. *Journal of Machine Accounting, Data Processing, Systems and Management*
   (monthly)
   1750 West Central Road
   Mount Prospect, Illinois
8. *Office Automation News Bulletin*
   155 Fifth Avenue
   New York 10, New York

BOOKS AND REPORTS

1. Canning, Sisson & Associates, *EDP Idea Finder,* Los Angeles, California,

1960. (Summaries of data processing articles and books, indexed by subject.)

2. Friedman, Burton D., *Punched Card Primer,* Public Administration Service, Chicago, Illinois, 1955.

3. Gallagher, James D., *Management Information Systems and the Computer,* American Management Association, New York, 1961.

4. Gregory, R. H., and R. L. Van Horn, *Automatic Data-processing Systems,* Second Edition, Wadsworth Publishing Company, San Francisco, California, 1963.

5. Haskins & Sells, *Introduction to Data Processing,* New York, 1957.

6. Ledley, R. S., *Programming and Utilizing Digital Computers,* McGraw-Hill Book Company, Inc., New York, 1962.

7. Lybrand, Ross Bros., and Montgomery Management Consulting Service, *Electronic Data Processing—Subject Bibliography of Periodical Literature—1960,* New York, 1961.

8. Martin, E. W., Jr., *Electronic Data Processing—An Introduction,* Richard Irwin, Inc., Homewood, Illinois, 1961.

9. Optner, S. L., *Systems Analysis for Business Management,* Prentice-Hall, Inc., Englewood Cliffs, New Jersey, 1960.

10. Postley, J. A., *Computers and People,* McGraw-Hill Book Company, Inc., New York, 1960.

11. Price Waterhouse & Company, *The Auditor Encounters Electronic Data Processing,* New York (n.d.).

12. Schmidt, R. N., and W. E. Meyers, *Electronic Business Data Processing,* Holt, Rinehart & Winston, Inc., New York, 1963.

13. Shultz, G. P., and T. L. Whisler (eds.), *Management Organization and the Computer,* The Free Press of Glencoe, Inc., New York, 1960.

14. Sprague, R. E., *Electronic Business Systems,* The Ronald Press Company, New York, 1962.

INDEX

The letter t preceding a page number indicates tabular material; numbers in boldface type indicate figures.

Selected RAND Books

Arrow, Kenneth J., and Marvin Hoffenberg, *A Time Series Analysis of Inter-industry Demands*. Amsterdam: North-Holland Publishing Company, 1959.

Bellman, Richard, *Adaptive Control Processes: A Guided Tour*. Princeton, N.J.: Princeton University Press, 1961.

Bellman, Richard (ed.), *Mathematical Optimization Techniques*. Berkeley and Los Angeles: University of California Press, 1963.

Bergson, Abram, *The Real National Income of Soviet Russia Since 1928*. Cambridge, Mass.: Harvard University Press, 1961.

Bergson, Abram, and Hans Heymann, Jr., *Soviet National Income and Product, 1940-48*. New York: Columbia University Press, 1954.

Buchheim, Robert W., and the Staff of The RAND Corporation, *Space Handbook: Astronautics and Its Applications*. New York: Random House, Inc., 1959.

Dorfman, Robert, Paul A. Samuelson, and Robert M. Solow, *Linear Programming and Economic Analysis*. New York: McGraw-Hill Book Company, Inc., 1958.

Dresher, Melvin, *Games of Strategy: Theory and Applications*. Englewood Cliffs, N.J.: Prentice-Hall, Inc., 1961.

Gale, David, *The Theory of Linear Economic Models*. New York: McGraw-Hill Book Company, Inc., 1960.

Galenson, Walter, *Labor Productivity in Soviet and American Industry*. New York: Columbia University Press, 1955.

Gouré, Leon, *Civil Defense in the Soviet Union*. Berkeley and Los Angeles: University of California Press, 1962.

Gruenberger, F. J., and D. D. McCracken, *Introduction to Electronic Computers*. New York: John Wiley & Sons, Inc., 1963.

Hastings, Cecil, Jr., *Approximations for Digital Computers*. Princeton, N.J.: Princeton University Press, 1955.

Hirshleifer, Jack, James C. DeHaven, and Jerome W. Milliman, *Water Supply: Economics, Technology, and Policy*. Chicago: The University of Chicago Press, 1960.

Hitch, Charles J., and Roland McKean, *The Economics of Defense in the Nuclear Age*. Cambridge, Mass.: Harvard University Press, 1960.

Hoeffding, Oleg, *Soviet National Income and Product in 1928.* New York: Columbia University Press, 1954.

Hsieh, Alice L., *Communist China's Strategy in the Nuclear Era.* Englewood Cliffs, N.J.: Prentice-Hall, Inc., 1962.

Kershaw, Joseph A., and Roland N. McKean, *Teacher Shortages and Salary Schedules.* New York: McGraw-Hill Book Company, Inc., 1962.

Lubell, Harold, *Middle East Oil Crises and Western Europe's Energy Supplies.* Baltimore, Maryland: The Johns Hopkins Press, 1963.

McKean, Roland N., *Efficiency in Government through Systems Analysis: With Emphasis on Water Resource Development.* New York: John Wiley & Sons, Inc., 1958.

Markowitz, H. M., B. Hausner, and H. W. Karr, *SIMSCRIPT: A Simulation Programming Language.* Englewood Cliffs, N.J.: Prentice-Hall, Inc., 1963.

Moorsteen, Richard, *Prices and Production of Machinery in the Soviet Union, 1928-1958.* Cambridge, Mass.: Harvard University Press, 1962.

Newell, Allen (ed.), *Information Processing Language-V Manual.* Englewood Cliffs, N.J.: Prentice-Hall, Inc., 1961.

Scitovsky, Tibor, Edward Shaw, and Lorie Tarshis, *Mobilizing Resources for War: The Economic Alternatives.* New York: McGraw-Hill Book Company, Inc., 1951.

Smith, Bruce Lannes, and Chitra M. Smith, *International Communication and Political Opinion: A Guide to the Literature.* Princeton, N.J.: Princeton University Press, 1956.

Sokolovskii, V. D., *Soviet Military Strategy.* Translated and annotated by H. S. Dinerstein, L. Gouré, and T. W. Wolfe. Englewood Cliffs, N.J.: Prentice-Hall, Inc., 1963.